Coaching Made Easier:
How to Successfully Manage Your
Youth Baseball Team

A Step-by-Step Guide to a Rewarding Season

Companion
CD-ROM
Included!

Rod Huff

COACHES
CHOICE™

ISBN: 978-1-60679-009-0
Library of Congress Control Number: 2008932153
Cover Design: Doug Powell and Studio J Art & Design
Book layout: Studio J Art & Design
Cover Photo: 2003 Sparrow Birds. Front Row (left to right): Matt Huff, Cody DeVault, John Michael Morris, Kevin Wieck, Austin Huff. Back Row (left to right): Coach Chuck Webb, Coach Glenn Hill, Matt Webb, John Greer, Spencer Hill, Blake Sullivan, Brent Adams, Coach Rod Huff. Not in Photo: Kyle Langley, Jonathan Miller, Kevin Nofi

Coaches Choice
P.O. Box 1828
Monterey, CA 93942
www.coacheschoice.com

Dedication

*"The difference between the impossible and the
possible lies in a man's determination."*

—Tommy Lasorda

This book is dedicated to my father, Earl Huff, who went to be with the Lord recently. He never missed one of my Little League games when I was playing, and I'm sorry that he isn't able to be here to celebrate this book. He was an inspiration to me as a dad, teaching me about life, work, fun, integrity, honesty, and things of the Lord. I miss my daily chats with him and the ability to share my life with him. He was a wonderful grandfather to all his grandchildren and always had a smile on his face. I know if he were still alive, he would be proud of my accomplishment of writing this book.

Earl K. Huff
August 28, 1923—October 12, 2005

Acknowledgments

"I can do all things through Him who strengthens me."

—Philippians 4:13

I would like to acknowledge the many people who encouraged me to put my methods and processes into a coaching book. My family, both immediate and extended, have been tremendously encouraging and supportive as I converted my ideas on coaching to the printed page. My wife, Lisa, a wonderful wife, a successful interior designer, and an incredible mom to our two children, Whitney and Austin, has been a tremendous help throughout the process. She was also the person who was my first editor and proofreader. My mother, Loyce, my brothers, Randy and Rick, and their families have all positively influenced the creative process behind this book.

In addition, to the countless number of parents who thanked me for the great experiences they had during the seasons. There are too many to list them all, but I would like to mention three families—the Webbs, the Hankses, and the Morrises. These families went above and beyond to encourage me and thank me for my efforts—I always did and still do appreciate them greatly.

No acknowledgment would be complete without mentioning my right-hand guy, Glenn Hill, who faithfully assisted me in my coaching experience for the entire history of the Birds. We complemented each other nicely and gave our players a balanced view on coaching. We were great partners—thanks, Glenn, for your help.

Then, to my friends outside of baseball, my Wednesday morning Bible study group—Norman Miller, Greg Nelson, David Hamilton, Neil Thrasher, Rick Horne, and, in the earlier days, Mike Glenn. We go through thick and thin together—thank you for always being there to build me up.

To a special friend from my days in the music business, Richard Green, who is the most entertaining lawyer I have ever met and a true friend—thanks for being who you are and looking so good in black. As he told me to say, this book would not have happened without him.

Most important, I thank our Lord, Jesus Christ, who has guarded my steps and blessed me with talent on the field and with the gift of writing. I am who I am as a result of His love for me.

Foreword

I have known Rod since the day we talked him into coaching (when his son was five), but I got to know him best as a coach during my five-year tenure as commissioner of Babe Ruth baseball for the 13- to 18-year-old age group in Brentwood, Tennessee. When I heard he was writing a book about youth sports programs, I was not surprised that he chose to focus on building relationships with the kids and managing a team of them. So many books have been published addressing skill development, technique, rules, and all of the technical aspects of youth sports performance, but I have yet to find one that addresses the pure and simple fundamentals of managing a team of young people. This topic is a neglected area in sports literature and an area that Rod addressed so effectively as a coach.

In my entire experience of administering baseball programs, I never met a coach who understood the big picture as well as Rod. He was a winner, without ever pressing kids to win. He created an environment on the field and in the dugout that inspired kids to love the sport and play like they loved it. His teams beat teams they shouldn't have beat. His teams outplayed teams that had more talent. His teams beat teams that were coached by more-experienced coaches. His teams beat teams that were coached by master tacticians. His teams beat teams that were driven in the "blood-and-guts" mode of their coaches. But, most important, his teams knew how to lose with grace. And at the end of the game or the end of the season, no matter what the outcome, they still loved the game. As a psychologist, I especially appreciated his talents in all aspects of managing a youth sports team. Children, and often their parents, can be enormously challenging from a managerial perspective. Rod's "management" of both was simply awesome.

Anyone who has ever assumed the daunting responsibility of running a baseball program knows that good coaches are hard to find. It was such a comfort to know that I could count on Rod returning every year. He set the standard for doing it right. Few achieve this level of insight, and I felt so fortunate to have one of them in my program.

I highly recommend that every aspiring coach, and indeed, every parent who has high hopes for their child's experience in organized sports get a copy of this book.

Dr. Frederick A. Ernst, Ph.D.
Tenured Professor of Psychology
Assistant Dean of Graduate Studies & Research
University of Texas-Pan American

Contents

Preface

Why Is There No Joy in Mudville?

*"Fear of failure must never be a reason
not to try something."*

—Frederick W. Smith, FedEx chairman, president, and CEO

There is no joy in Mudville, and it's not because the mighty Casey struck out. The lack of joy is because so many young baseball players around the country are having bad experiences in baseball. The leaders of the leagues are just happy to have warm bodies that are willing to volunteer. No one takes the time to teach the volunteers how to coach, so they fumble through the season, attempting to make the best of the situation. Ironically, most of these new coaches do not even realize that they are not being good coaches. Typically, the only judge of their effectiveness rests in their win-loss records. The purpose of this book is to provide greater meaning to the coaching experience by equipping you, as a volunteer coach, to handle the day-to-day management of your team.

When I first became a coach, I searched for books on baseball coaching. What I found was a plethora of books on baseball instruction—books that taught general baseball skills such as hitting, pitching, etc. I did not find any books on what it actually takes to manage a team, the players, and the parents. Through trial and error over the years, I have developed an effective way to manage the process of coaching youth baseball teams.

My method is a combination of business management and basic teaching skills. An overriding twofold principle, which is paramount to successful youth baseball coaching, is a love of young people and a love of the game of baseball. The absence of either of these two elements will cause the methods in this book to fall short.

I was unaware that I had stumbled onto anything special until I reflected on the success of my teams after 11 years of coaching. For 9 of the 11 years, I was the head coach. By typical measurements of wins and losses, I had been successful. In the nine years as head coach, I had won five league championships and one postseason tournament, and was runner-up in four others. My team, the Sparrow Records Birds, had achieved a reputation throughout our community as being the team to beat. Many players throughout the league could tell you what their records were against the Birds.

In our particular league, with the exception of their own children, the coaches had to draft an entirely new team each season. Our teams had to be built anew each year. Despite this fact, we continued to have winning seasons every year.

As stated previously, having a winning season does not necessarily make you a successful coach. More important than our win-loss record was the fact that parents would call me and ask me to draft their child. At our end-of-the-year team parties, parents would shower me with compliments, and I was told many times that their child had the best coaching experience of his life. When it first started to happen, I was shocked, not realizing that I was doing anything different. However, I started to observe how my son's other coaches (soccer, football, and basketball) handled their teams, and our styles were distinctively different. I am a very modest individual who is not good at receiving praise. I always try to give credit to God and my assistant coaches before even considering accepting it on my behalf. During this time, I did develop a passion for coaching and a desire to share my "system" with other coaches.

I do things differently, and I think this approach will work for other coaches, providing they have the love of young people and the game of baseball. The purpose of this book is to share my coaching "secrets" with other coaches. As you will see as you read through the pages of this book, this system is nothing magical or mystical. These are basic suggestions that will have you saying, "Why didn't I think of that?"

My players loved coming to practices and games. By the end of every season, we were melded into a team, and we were all sad when it was over. If you are looking for a book filled with methods to teach skills, this book is not for you. If you think you are already a great coach or don't think you have anything to learn about coaching, this book is not for you. If you are interested in improving your coaching and team management skills, having your players truly enjoy their experience, having the parents of your players sing your praises, and, at the same time, improving your win-loss records, then read on.

About the Companion CD-ROM

The CD-ROM that accompanies this book provides administrative aids and various tools that can help make your coaching experience more enjoyable. A basic knowledge of Microsoft Office suite products is desirable, but not a requirement to utilize these tools. If using a computer is not within your particular skill set, your assistant coach or a parent volunteer may be able to assist in this aspect of the suggested administrative duties of coaching.

The CD-ROM includes two types of files: "templates" and "examples." A roster template is organized to allow you to insert information about your team and use that information in various ways to create worksheets that can assist you in managing your team. A scrapbook template is included to give you a framework upon which to build a keepsake-like scrapbook for your players and supporters. Also included is a template that will assist you in conducting a draft if you get tapped to manage a league or an age group in your league.

The "examples" are sample handouts, agendas, etc. that you can utilize as illustrations to create your own documents. They can also be used by cutting and pasting your information into the documents.

Best of luck with your coaching experience! Visit our website www.CoachingMadeEasier.net for more helpful hints.

1

Good Teams Are Never an Accident

"Individual commitment to a group effort—that is what makes a team work, a company work, a society work, a civilization work."

—Vince Lombardi

This chapter will take you through the fundamentals of getting started as a coach, from the draft to your first practice and parents meeting. The processes outlined in this chapter should not be taken lightly—mistakes made in the early pre-season can be difficult to correct as the season progresses.

The Draft

As a new coach, the first challenge will be the annual draft of players. Procedures on how leagues draft their teams vary from league to league. Whether your league requires you to redraft your team each year or allows you to freeze players and only draft to fill the holes left by players moving on, the following techniques and tips will apply.

Drafting a team can be a daunting experience. The process often begins by taking a clipboard to the field and judging all the prospective players. Tryout methods will vary, but generally, you are asked to assign a numerical evaluation to each player's hitting, fielding, throwing, and (in the older-age groups) pitching abilities.

Rating players is highly subjective. Nevertheless, at the end of the day all the numbers are crunched, and the players are sorted in descending order from who received the highest rating at tryouts to who received the lowest rating. That list is sensitive for obvious reasons, and it is usually collected from the coaches following the draft. In addition to how the players were rated in hitting, fielding, throwing, pitching, and an overall rating, the list includes information about the age and prior experience of the player.

Along with the objective criteria that show up on the report, you should be aware of subjective issues as well. Knowledge of the players' families, whether they have older siblings, etc. can be used for this analysis. You should use caution since players with bad attitudes can try out and score very high. As you continue coaching, the names of players to avoid will become familiar. Until you gather the experience, you have to rely on your knowledge of the community. If your league allows your assistant coach to participate, use him. The more collective knowledge about the players you have, the better off you will be. Your assistant may know things, good or bad, about some of the players that you do not know. More knowledge is always better—especially in the subjective arena.

Leagues usually provide time for you and your assistant coach to review the list prior to beginning the draft. During that time, review the list thoroughly, and highlight the names of players you would like to have on your team. Look for the diamonds in the rough. Strong players may not always do well during tryouts. Tryouts usually take place in the early spring when the weather is typically cold, and many of the players may not have touched their bats or gloves since the previous summer. Look for the gems who did not perform well at tryouts. Use knowledge that you or your assistant may have regarding the player's athletic skills in other sports. In the early age groups, a boy who is good in one sport will typically be good in other sports. Birth order is also important—players who have older brothers tend to be advanced in sports for their age.

As you coach more, you will begin to recognize the names of players you had previously or ones who played well against you in prior seasons. Pick those players as soon as possible—don't wait simply because they are down lower in the draft. Other coaches may have made the same observations, and an observant coach might snag a player long before what his draft rating would warrant. Do not waste a first or second-round choice, but always try to draft the hidden gems prior to the round in which they would normally be selected.

Do not simply look at the overall rating—look for a well-rounded player. For example, the overall rating of a player who lacks fielding skills may be skewed due to his talent as a hitter. These situations are rare, but they can hurt you in the draft if you are not careful. Pay particular attention to the pitching rating. Pitchers are extremely important to youth baseball teams. It is difficult to win a lot of games with only one pitcher. All youth leagues have restrictions to protect overzealous coaches from overpitching young players. Make sure you draft two or three players who scored high in the pitching evaluations.

When it gets down to drafting players that you and your assistant don't know anything about (beyond what is on the paper), you should rely on two factors: their parents and the age of the player. Another option, if permitted, would be to ask one of your own children about unknown players. It's surprising how much insight you can gain from your children in these situations. The athletes and well-behaved kids are known by their classmates.

If you know the parents and think they would be strong supporters of your team, 9 times out of 10 their child will be an asset to your team. It is important to consider who the parents of the players are when drafting your team. Parents who will strongly support your program are worth their weight in gold.

The age factor may seem like a given, but it's surprising how often coaches fail to pay attention to the age column on the draft sheets. Generally, youth baseball is divided into age brackets of two years each. Depending on the age group, a substantial difference exists between the lower and upper ages. This discrepancy is especially apparent when you get into the 11- to 12-year-old age group. If everything else is equal, go with the older player.

Once the draft is behind you, pull your team together as soon as possible and start practicing. You have the players that have been dealt to you—it's time to start forming this ragtag group of draftees into a cohesive baseball team.

The First Practice

Never set out to accomplish much from a skills point of view at your first practice. In fact, do not spend any time at all *teaching* the players anything. The things you should hope to accomplish are: getting to know the players, having the players meet each other, getting a rough idea of their fielding skills, and most important, having a formal meeting with the parents.

A spreadsheet should be developed to track your players through spring training (Figure 1-1*). Keep track of the players' pre-season attendance as well as their desires and progress made during the practices. When your players arrive at that first practice, introduce yourself and pair them with another player or two to play catch. Have one player stand near the first or third base line and have their partner in right or left field. This positioning allows the players to loosen up their arms and begin to warm up. Get them in the habit of getting in this formation as it will be the way you begin each practice and game.

*To add a degree of professionalism to all reports and handouts, include a logo of your team mascot or your sponsor. To illustrate this concept, the figures in this book feature a logo for the fictional sponsor ABC Records & Publishing.

ABC Birds Pre-Season Attendance
2008 Brentwood Baseball Babe Ruth League

Manager - Rod Huff — 555-4340
Coach - Glenn Hill — 555-7741
Coach - Chuck Webb — 555-3125

Player Name	#	Best Times		Position	Parents	Phone #	3/10	3/13	3/17	3/18	3/20	3/24	3/25	3/27	3/31	4/1	4/3	4/7	4/8	4/14	4/15	4/17
		H-1st	1st-2nd									Spring Break	Spring Break	Spring Break		Canceled						
Paul Abraham	8	4.91	4.80	P,SS,2B	Bill/Lydia	555-6789	X	X	X	X	X				X		X	X	X	X	X	X
Jake Beam	6	5.66	5.47	C,1B	Chuck/Julia	555-3125	X	X	X	X	X				X		X	X	X	X	X	X
Keith Green	21	4.75	4.79	3B,SS,OF	Cady/Kim	555-7845	X		X	X	X				X						X	X
Spencer Hill	00	4.50	4.60	P,1B,OF	Glenn/Vickie	555-7741	X	X	X	X	X				X							
Austin Huff	34	4.03	4.15	CF,2B,SS,C	Rod/Lisa	555-4340		X		X	X				X		X	X	X	X		X
Matt Haines	22	4.86	4.65	C,P,IN	Craig/Melanie	555-5260	X	X	X	X					X		X	X	X	X		X
Neal Joseph	45	5.12	5.16	OF,P	Hal/Martha	555-9870	X	X	X	X	X				X		X	X	X	X		X
John Knight	5	5.02	4.88	3B,SS	Joe/Carol	555-4279	X	X	X	X	X				X		X	X				
Norman Miller	15	4.10	4.16	P,1B,OF	John/Elizabeth	555-1234	X	X	X	X	X				X		X	X	X	X	X	
Micky Norris	3	4.88	5.10	C,P,IN	Kent/Donna	555-4332	X	X	X	X	X				X							X
Bill Phillips	17	4.25	4.27	OF,P	Peter/Nancy	555-1991	X	X	X	X	X				X							
Matt Ross	14	4.33	4.43	3B,SS	Eddie/Nancy	555-1478	X	X	X	X	X				X		X	X	X	X		X
John Webb	23	4.30	4.51	P,1B,OF	Chuck/Lisa	555-3125	X	X	X	X	X				X		X	X	X		X	X
Totals							11	10	10	11	11	0	0	0	13	0	9	9	7	6	3	7
Average Times		4.67	4.69																			

NOTE: Positions are the positions they prefer to play

ABC Records & Publishing

Figure 1-1. Pre-season attendance chart

As the team is warming up, walk around and have a "meeting" with each player. Introduce yourself and tell the player what you prefer to be called (i.e., Coach Smith or Coach Bob). During these meetings, get down on a knee and talk eye-to-eye with the younger players (as you coach in the teenage years, you'll find yourself having to look up to your players). This point may seem insignificant, but it's important that a coach does not look down on his players. By taking the eye-to-eye approach, you relieve some of the anxiety of your first meeting, and you can accomplish much more from the start.

During these first meetings, try to find out more about the players than what you were able to learn from the draft sheets. Ask them questions like, "If you could play any position, what would it be?" Note their answers on the sheets and keep them with you during the entire pre-season. Of course, it's not always possible to put a player in his favorite position. However, you will find that players who do get the opportunity to play in their desired positions—at least occasionally throughout the year—have a much more positive experience. If a coach doesn't ask that question, he may never know the player's desires.

Use your one-on-one time to find out more information about the player, such as the size of his family, where he attends school, how many years he has played the game, etc. This time is valuable—never underestimate its value in laying the foundation of your team.

To find out the speed of your base runners, it is important to time each player's run from home plate to first base and first base to second base. This exercise doesn't necessarily have to take place during the first practice, but it should be done no later than the second practice. Log the times on your pre-season chart. Make a game out of timing their base running and do it often throughout the pre-season. Be sure to inform the players when they improve their times. Players appreciate this feedback and they make it a competition among the other players and, more important, with themselves in an effort to improve their times.

Conclude your first practice by hitting grounders. Have the entire team line up at shortstop and second base, and rotate the players who expressed an interest in playing first base to that position. The purpose of this exercise is to get a rough idea of the fielding and throwing abilities of the team. It also gives you a general feel of which players need remedial help with some of the basics.

Ask the parents to show up approximately 15 minutes prior to the conclusion of practice for a meeting. While you are meeting with the parents, ask your assistant coach to continue to hit grounders, and conclude with a team meeting to see if any of the players can name everyone else on the team. Reward anyone who can name all the players with a pack of baseball cards.

Baseball cards are great motivators, and you will see as you read on how you can use them throughout the season. During the pre-season, you can play games such as the familiar egg toss, and the two players left would receive cards, or you can run races around the outfield with the winner getting a pack of cards, etc. Details of these and other ideas can be found in Chapter 2.

The first practice is concluded with the players getting the handout "How to Look Like a Baseball Player" (Figure 1-2)—the first in a series of handouts. Stress the importance of this handout and remind them throughout the season of the importance of appearance in relation to the way they play the game. The traditions of baseball are strong. Set standards based on this handout early on. Once left unchecked, it's difficult to get the horse back in the barn, so to speak. Things like wearing hats backward and leaving shirttails out should not be tolerated once practice begins. As the season progresses, you may see players showing up at practices and games wearing something other than a team hat—do not allow this habit to form. If you do, your team will quickly look unkempt, which contributes to a team that is undisciplined. *Team* means that everyone looks alike, including headwear and socks. Make sure your league provides a few extras of those items for situations when a player loses a piece of his uniform.

The Parents Meeting

The most important part of your first practice should be the time you spend in your parents meeting. In most cases, you will be meeting the parents of your players for the first time. As the saying goes, you only have one chance to make a first impression. Remember that concept as you prepare for the meeting—take the necessary time in preparation, and know what you hope to accomplish. You will have time as the season progresses to learn about each of your parents, so use this time to present yourself to them.

Share your coaching philosophy so they know what to expect as the season goes on. If you are new to coaching or you have not yet developed your own coaching philosophy, this book may help you to do so. Prepare a formal agenda to help the parents follow along during the meeting and to insure that you do not miss anything important that you had planned to discuss (Figure 1-3). You should also write a letter that summarizes your discussion for any parents who cannot make the meeting and so the parents that were present will have a reminder of what you discussed (Figure 1-4). You will learn that you cannot overcommunicate. No matter how many times you say something or provide handouts, certain players or parents will always claim they never got the message.

Attempt to make your handouts and communications that go to the parents look as professional as possible. This point will be readdressed in Chapter 6. Things such as creating your handouts on a computer or adding a logo from your sponsor or team to

ABC
Records & Publishing

How to Look Like a Baseball Player

◊ Never sit down on the field or on a base.

◊ Always hustle on every play.

◊ Always run on and off the field between innings.

◊ Do not play in the dirt.

◊ Never show your anger or frustration.

◊ Keep track of the score, how many runners are on base, and how many outs there are at all times.

◊ Do not wear your hat backward in a non-rally-cap situation.

◊ Always wear your hat and shirt when you are on the field.

◊ Do not ignore the game when you're on the bench.

◊ Always look neat with shirttail tucked in.

◊ Never let striking out or making an error distract you so that you make more mistakes.

◊ Never argue with the umpire, your coach, or another player.

Figure 1-2. How to look like a baseball player

ABC
Records & Publishing

PARENTS' MEETING AGENDA

March 3, 2008

◊ Introductions

◊ Coaching Philosophy
- Skill Goals
- Statistics
- Positive Interactions
- Game Balls
- Punctuality/Missed Games
- Having Fun Is #1

◊ Parental Involvement/Volunteers

◊ Team Roster

◊ Schedule

◊ Important Phone Numbers
- Field Rain Hotline 555-8310
- Coach Rod 555-4340 (H) 555-6806 (O)
- Coach Glenn 555-7741 (H) 555-8550 (O)
- Coach Chuck 555-3125 (H) 555-1088 (O)

◊ Questions and Answers

Figure 1-3. Parents' meeting agenda

your handouts are all things that parents are probably not used to seeing from volunteer coaches, and it adds an element of credibility and professionalism from the start.

Consider the things that you want the parents to buy into and present them at this meeting. For example, some coaches make it a practice to pray before each game. Being sensitive to our politically-correct society, let the parents know if you prefer to do something of this nature, and ask that they talk with you if they have any objections. Promote discussions on these topics so the parents do not feel like they have been railroaded into anything.

This meeting is the ideal time to present opportunities for parents to get involved in your season and lay out the general job descriptions for each position. Some positions are essential for your team's success while others are simply important. Every job needs to be taken seriously by the individual who steps up. Job requirements and even the jobs need to be changed as your players get older. The following jobs are generally what you should attempt to fill during the early part of the pre-season.

Assistant Coach: A good assistant coach should complement you in many ways. Therefore, it is important to identify your strengths and weaknesses before you recruit for this position. For instance, if you are not administratively gifted, look for an assistant who has administrative skills. Or perhaps you know a parent in the league who played baseball in college and would be strong in the skills department. Search out the right person for this position. Most leagues allow you to pair up before the season starts, which gives you more of a pool to draw from than simply having to choose from the parents of the players you drafted. Selecting your assistant before the draft also guarantees that his son will be protected in the draft. You will be working very closely with this person for the entire season, so make sure that your personalities do not collide. The spirit of team must be a top priority and having a pair of coaches who are compatible makes the job of forming a team much easier.

Second Assistant Coach: Most leagues allow for one head coach and two assistants. The job description of the second assistant should be patterned based on your skills and the skills of your assistant. For instance, if neither you nor your assistant coach are skilled in the pitching area, you should try to find a parent with pitching skills—not always possible, but always a good thought. Having an official second assistant position keeps the question of who will be in the dugout clear to some zealous dads on game day. However, at practice, you should always welcome any dad or mom who is observing to take an active role if they are interested. Five or six coaches doing different drills is not too many, especially in the early pre-season practices.

ABC
Records & Publishing

March 3, 2008

Dear Parents,

Thanks for allowing your son to participate with our team in this year's Babe Ruth Baseball League. Our team is sponsored by ABC Records & Publishing, a contemporary Christian music company with headquarters here in Brentwood. Our biggest goal for the year will be that your son has a fun and rewarding experience. In doing so, we hope to create an environment in which your son will increase his knowledge of the basics and fundamentals of baseball with a heavy emphasis on sportsmanship, attitude, and integrity.

As adults, we all need to set an example that will assist the other coaches and me in accomplishing our goals. The umpires will be professional TSSAA umpires, but they will most likely make mistakes in their calls—please refrain from making issues of their mistakes. We all want to win games, but we also want to ensure that we set good examples and role models for our players while having as much fun as possible.

This year, Brentwood Babe Ruth Baseball is trying something new. For the first time ever, last year's 14 year olds who played for ABC are returning to ABC. In years past, new drafts took place each year. Prior to this year, teams were broken up and rebuilt with new players annually. We have eight players who played on the team last year as 14 year olds. I want to reassure all new members of the team that there will not be preferential treatment to the boys who played last year and that no position has been assigned and/or guaranteed to anyone. The coaching staff will make those determinations throughout our pre-season practices and games.

In regard to our season, our first game will be Monday, April 21 vs. Team #3. Following spring break, we will try to practice three times each week. In addition to fields #2 and #3 at Granny White Park, we will have the use of the field at Cumberland Presbyterian Church on Franklin Road in Brentwood. Since the church field is actually a softball diamond, we will use that time to run drills. Our season will consist of three games against each of the other six teams.

Every season, it seems that our teams really come together as we come down the home stretch in June. If at all possible, I encourage you not to schedule vacations prior to the July 4 holiday. This will ensure that our team will stay together through the tournament. There's nothing worse for a team than to be broken up prior to the tournament due to a trip to "Gram and Pap's" by one of our key players. Thanks in advance for considering this as you make your summer plans.

During the course of the season, you may at times become overwhelmed with the amount of handouts your son brings home. At nearly every practice or game, I attempt to

Figure 1-4. Parents letter

give him the next two or three scheduled events. Knowing 14- to 15-year-old boys, I realize that they do not always give their parents what they're supposed to. Ask them to make sure they relay all handouts on to you. This is how we will communicate with you throughout the season. I will always attempt to copy these handouts on a very bright paper stock so that when they get crumpled at the bottoms of the players' baseball bags, you can spot them more easily.

As we begin our games, the boys will receive complete stats. I will put a three-hole punch in these, and I suggest that you get a notebook to save them. The boys usually treasure their stats and like to keep them. I use them to establish my lineups and generally manage the team. I've also found that the boys are motivated to improve on their statistics. Please encourage this practice, and ask them how they're doing from time to time.

Glenn and I have been coaching the Birds together now for eight years, and Chuck has been a part of our team for four years. We do have winning seasons with a winning percentage of over 70%. We will be attempting to have win number 100 this season. Winning, however, has never been our primary focus. Our first wish is that the boys have a fun environment to learn baseball skills and to give them the opportunity to excel. You will hear your son talk about a team goal that we will have this year, challenging every member of the team to get to and win the championship game of the league. Over the past nine years, the Birds have won five league championships and have been runner-up in another three seasons. There was only one year that we were not either champion or runner-up. The boys refer to that as the "purple year," since that was the only year we switched from our traditional teal jerseys to purple. I'm not the superstitious type but...this year, we're taking purple out of our uniforms altogether. Winning the championship will be our major goal, but along the way we will have many other goals—some individual and some team-oriented. I ask for your encouragement in this process.

We have been blessed over the years with a tremendous amount of parental support during the games and as volunteers. We have the following opportunities for assistance:

- **Scorekeeper:** This person will assist in the coaching duties during practices and pre-game warm-ups. This is a key member of the team and critical to my ability to deliver statistics to the boys. You are not required to be at practices or even every game. I do ask that this person assume responsibility for finding someone who can keep the score book for us if he/she can not be at a game.

- **Team Mom/Dad/Couple:** This person will be responsible for coordinating various activities throughout the season, such as team parties, trophies (if we do not finish in a position that we will win trophies—only division winners, tournament winners, and runners-up win trophies provided by Brentwood Baseball), etc. This is a key position and critical to the formation of the team.

Each of these positions will have the responsibility throughout the season, which begins April 21 and runs until the end of June. I'd like to try to have a team sleepover if some brave parent is willing to step up to the challenge prior to our first game.

Please contact me if you are interested in helping us out. You can reach me, Rod Huff, at 555-4340, or during working hours, my office number is 555-6806, or I always have a cell phone with me 555-7233. My assistant coaches are Glenn Hill, who can be reached at 555-7741, and Chuck Webb at 555-3125.

PLAY BALL!

Figure 1-4. cont.

Dugout Coach: This position is no longer needed after the 12-year-old season, and the person who steps up is often referred to as the bravest volunteer on your staff. They help keep the batting order flowing, keep gloves and hats matched to kids and, in general, act as the disciplinarian of the dugout. You should refer to them as Coach, and reinforce whatever action they deem appropriate to keep order in the dugout. They are a key member of your coaching staff.

Team Mom or Dad: This position is delegated the responsibility for all nongame activities such as: coordinating team parties, organizing game snacks, etc. When recruiting for what may seem like a mundane position, you should establish how important this position is—it is a key element in pulling a group of kids who don't all know each other together as a cohesive team by the conclusion of the season. A weak team mom or dad can make for a long season for the players and the coaches. You do not want to have to worry about details such as parties and snacks as they distract from your main focus of molding and shaping baseball players.

Scorekeeper: As you will see as you dig deeper into the coaching philosophy presented in this book, a great deal of importance is placed on this position. Statistics are *the key* to successfully managing your team and the major differentiator between you and the coach in the opposing dugout. A fairly decent knowledge of baseball is required for this job. Actual scorekeeping shorthand can be taught, but the intricacies of the game must be well understood. You should also attach another important element to this position. It is this person's responsibility to keep the official score book at every game, and if he cannot make it to a game, it is *his* responsibility to find a substitute.

Always stress in your meeting that the most important thing for the season is that everyone, including the parents, have a fun, rewarding experience. This pre-season meeting sets the tone and creates a respect level for you as head coach that must be established early in the process. You are the coach and they are the parents—each has a role in a successful season on and off the field.

Communication is a major key to the coach receiving parental support. This meeting should be the first—not the only—communication that you have with your parents. Communication is so important that much of Chapter 6 will be dedicated to the topic.

Wrap-Up

Your first job as a coach will be to draft your team. Remember to carefully review the information your league gives you from the tryouts. Do not look at just the players' rating totals on the sheet—players may be gifted in one aspect of the game and weak in others. A high total could easily be skewed.

When in doubt, draft the older boys in a league that spans a two-year window. Draft for parents as well as players. If you are aware of a supportive parent, you will tend to find their children easier to coach. Children with athletic older brothers are a fairly safe bet.

Be careful, take your time, and solicit all the information that is available to you, including asking your own children for input if allowed by your league. You will be surprised by how much they can help in the process.

Take extra time in preparing for your first practice—you have only one chance to make that first impression. Have a well-organized, professional meeting with the parents toward the end of your first practice. Share your philosophy, and leave them with a letter that restates everything you discussed with them. This step is the first, and possibly the most important, step in setting up good lines of communication with your parents. Managed properly, your parents will be a big support to you during the season. Examine Chapter 6 for more information regarding keeping your parents on your side.

Now, you have drafted a team that runs the gamut from gifted athletes to first-year players. Your work is cut out for you as you take this ragtag group of players and mold them into a team—ideally a team that they are proud to be a part of. Teams that are good are not created by accident. Creating a strong team takes the *seven Ps of team building*: planning, preparation, persistence, patience, perspiration, practice, and principle (Figure 1-5). The following chapters will touch on all seven of the *Ps*. Following the steps outlined in this book will result in the formation of a team that your players and parents will recall with fond memories.

With your first practice and your first parents meeting under your belt, it's time to get started. You are off on the right foot, but your work has only begun. The next chapter takes a look at the basic structure of your pre-season plan and practice structure as you prepare for that all-important first game.

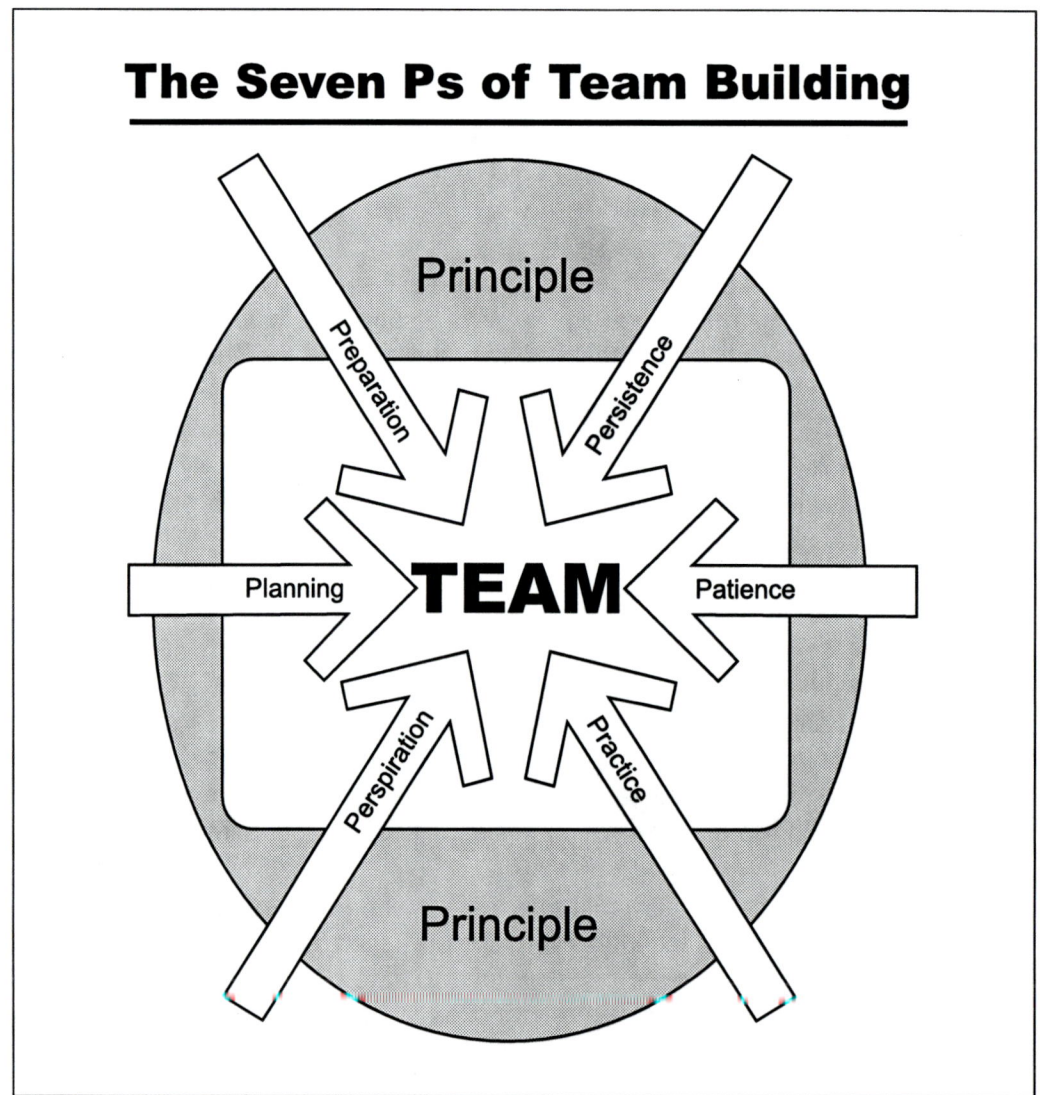

Figure 1-5. The seven Ps of team building

A Draft Accomplishment

As you start a new season, you never know exactly what is in store for you and your team. I'll never forget one season when we had come down to the final draft choice, and we were in a position to have the last pick. In other words, we were *stuck* with what was left. The better players had been chosen and it came down to our last selection. We had a choice to make between a player who had a reputation as being a troublemaker and a player who was entering into his first season at an age when other players had six to eight years of experience playing baseball.

It appeared to be trouble either way for me—a troublemaker or a player who would require a lot of extra work. The coach before me drafted "trouble," leaving me faced with the challenge of teaching baseball basics, including the fundamental rules, to a 14-year-old young man.

I was concerned about the extra burden of working with a player who was starting his baseball career so late compared to the other players. Our coaches and even the other players accepted the challenge and welcomed Paul (a fictitious name, as are all names in this book) with open arms. What had concerned me as a possible detriment to our team turned out to be a rallying point around which our whole team focused. As the season got under way, the parents joined our efforts by cheering for Paul as he came to the plate. It took several games, but Paul finally made contact at the plate and reached first base on a bloop single to right field. The team and the crowd went crazy—you would have thought we had just won the league title. Spectators from other games at the park were looking over to our field to see what happened.

One of the fondest memories from my coaching experience is seeing the expression on Paul's face as he hustled down the first base line. He was beaming from ear to ear—a moment I still hold precious. Always try to make the best of any situation that comes your way. Paul turned into a reliable hitter in our lineup and was a wonderful addition to our team. It took patience and the assistance of all the coaches and the players to chip in and help Paul. However, the time paid off and Paul became a welcomed addition to the Birds that year.

2

You Play Like You Practice

"The will to win is important, but the will to prepare is vital."

—Joe Paterno

The old adage is true—practice *does* make perfect—and it is no exception in youth baseball. The better prepared your team is, the better they will perform, the more fun they will have, and the happier the parents will be. These three components constitute a successful team. Like a stool with only three legs, if one element is missing, your team can not stand.

Another cliché that you may hear being used on the baseball diamond, the soccer field, the football field, the basketball court, or any other organized sports arena is: you play like you practice. As the coach, you must instill this principle in the minds of your players. The harder they work at practice, the better they will be—and the better they are, the better the team will be.

The age group you are coaching will present its own set of unique challenges. At the younger ages, your biggest challenge will be getting the players to focus on baseball rather than the infield dirt. As the players get older, their focus may be on the giggling girls at the practice field. Whatever the distractions may be, it is the job of the coaching staff to keep the team's attention. This chapter presents suggestions to assist you in conducting successful practices.

Building a Team

During the first few practices, it is important to establish the ground rules while your team is still getting to know you and each other. Often, your players begin the season as complete strangers. Some of them may know a few of the other players but not all of them. The natural tendency is for the players who know each other to congregate, and if this habit goes unchecked, your team will consist of several cliques rather than being one *team*.

As a coach, you can do a couple of things to guard against this type of behavior. First, take the time at each practice to have a team meeting. Have the players take a knee as you talk to them about various aspects of the game. Establish a rule that at these meetings every player looks at you while you are speaking. This rule may sound elementary, but minds can wander and requiring your players to make eye contact is an excellent way to know you have their attention.

To insure that cliques do not develop and that all the players know each other, have them introduce themselves to the team at your first practice, during the team meeting. In the 12 and under age groups, playing games is a good way to help them remember everyone's names. Offer a small prize to any player who can go around the group and identify every player by name. Baseball cards are an excellent incentive. Cards from previous seasons can be purchased at discount stores, and packs can be broken into individual cards to cut down on the expense. Play this game until you are certain that all the players know each other by name. This game is also a good way for the coaches to learn names.

Knowing names is the first step in teambuilding. As practice plans are developed, be aware of the kids who know each other well, and mix them up when you break your team down into smaller groups to work on drills. The more interaction new teammates can have together, the better off you and your team will be.

A divisive element in the creation of *team* is when players, usually the more talented players, feel compelled to "coach" their teammates. From day one, you must insist that only the coaches do the coaching. Have a rule that players are only allowed to make positive comments to fellow players. This rule may sound like logical advice that would be easy to implement. It is logical—it is not easy to enforce. You and your coaches will have to police this type of behavior. Warnings and disciplinary measures such as taking laps around the field or sitting out of fun drills are effective and will likely be required, but consistency is the key. Nip this behavior early in the pre-season and it should not become a problem as the season progresses.

This same principle applies as you face other teams and umpires in games. Making derogatory comments about players on other teams can not be tolerated. Encourage your team to embrace the concept of the golden rule—*do unto others as you would have them do unto you*. As part of the instruction and discipline, have your players visualize themselves in the other players' shoes, and ask them to imagine how negative comments would make them feel. Taking a hard line on this kind of behavior early will reap major benefits as you build your team. Your team will embrace this concept, and the players will begin to police themselves. Peer pressure will align with what you are trying to achieve, and your team will begin to pull together.

As the season gets underway and once you have laid the groundwork that the coach is the *only* authority on the team and the *only* spokesperson, it is easier for the players to understand that no one ever discusses anything with the umpires except for one of the coaches. You will want to have an understanding with each of your assistant coaches that your team does not make a practice of disputing umpires' calls. This topic will be discussed in more detail in Chapter 3. Your attitude and the way you interact with other coaches and umpires sets the tone for how your players and parents will relate to and show respect toward those positions. *Respect* must be the key word in all your dealings.

As *team* is developed and the players get to know each other better, it is good to do something with them outside of practice. A Saturday afternoon movie, a pizza party, laser tag, or any other activity will help them develop relationships that will bond them. Activities involving parents are excellent as they will be your support team throughout the season. The sooner they get to know each other, the better for you as you prepare to begin your season. When relationships develop among your players' parents, they are more apt to come to the games and support your team. Your players will respond positively to cheering fans.

How Often Do We Practice?

The question of how many times per week to practice is a tricky one. It's true that the more you practice, the better your team will be. However, young ball players have limited attention spans. Coaches who practice excessively often find that their teams lose interest during practices—especially toward the end of the season. On the flip side, coaches who do not practice often enough find difficulty getting wins. The concept of quantity versus quality applies in this case. The key is having quality practice sessions, often enough to separate you from the rest of the teams.

Leagues usually allocate practice times in the pre-season based on the number of teams and the availability of fields. One thing that you can usually count on is that there will be limited field time available. Get creative and search for other fields that your team can use.

Teams in the younger age brackets can use a large yard or vacant field almost anywhere. Be aware that the other coaches will likely limit their practice times to what was assigned by the league, so you can differentiate your team simply by having one more practice time per week than the other teams. You will be surprised by the way this additional practice time benefits your team and separates your team from the pack.

Look around your community for ballfields. Incidentally, softball fields can work just as well for the 12 and under teams. For the older players, if a softball field is all that you have available, you can make it work by setting up your practice to do drills or conditioning that will work on a field that is not an official baseball diamond. Fly-ball drills for player positioning, rundown or pickle drills, base running drills, and various other drills can all be adapted to fields that do not have the official dimensions.

Churches, schools, or community parks often have fields that can be reserved for little or no money. Securing a reservation when planning practices at other fields is important—you lose credibility if your team and parents show up to an occupied field. Maintaining control of your players is difficult enough while they are on the field— maintaining control along the outside of a field while you wait for another team to conclude can be nearly impossible. A simple reservation insures you of the use of a field at a designated time, and it gives you the authority to have a squatter move on.

Before holding a practice elsewhere, double-check with your league to make sure their liability insurance covers your team at non-league fields. Although typically they will, it is better to have this information in advance. Often, the organization making the reservation for you will require proof of insurance before they allow you to use their field.

Another argument for finding an alternative practice field is the weather. Spring, in most parts of the country, is a volatile time of year in regard to the weather. The first game is scheduled and will be played regardless of the number of practices that you were able to have. If all but one of your regularly scheduled practices were rained out, you will take on your first opponent at a distinct disadvantage. This example may seem extreme, but it happens more often than you might think. Extra field time improves your odds of putting together a team that knows what is happening in their first real game.

Another advantage of locating an alternate practice field is that the league-designated practice times often disappear after the season begins. The league uses their fields for games and make-up games and does not usually have times available for practices. Practices that you are able to get in during the season help your team stay sharp between games. They also give you the opportunity to work on the fine points of the sport, the weak points of your team, and the strategy of the game.

There is no absolute right answer to the question of how often to practice your team. Every team requires different amounts of coaching and attention. Play it by ear, but leave your options open.

Keep attendance on the pre-season spreadsheet (Figure 1-1). This chart may help you realize which players are going to be dedicated to your team. Call the players who do not show up to find out why they missed. Early season no-shows may indicate that a player has changed his mind about playing. Acquiring this information early could allow you the opportunity to pick up a replacement player who was late signing up. The exercise of calling also lets the parents know that you expect the players to attend every practice. Find ways to reward those players who have good attendance records in the pre-season practices. You are aiming to have a team that is better prepared than every opponent. To reach this goal, full participation is required.

Safety

As the coach, when you are conducting a practice, you may be the only person with any authority at the field. The responsibility for maintaining a safe environment for your players rests squarely on your shoulders. Always be prepared for the inevitable accident. Although you pray that it will never happen, the chances are that, during your season, you will experience at least a few minor accidents—scrapes, bruises, etc. Along with your baseball equipment, always have a fully stocked first-aid kit and a small cooler filled with ice. It is also imperative that you have access to a phone in the event of a more serious accident.

Plan your practices with safety in mind. Regardless of the age of your players, make sure that the first thing on your practice schedule involves some stretching. Obviously, stretching becomes more important in the older age groups, but it is a good habit to get into before every practice and game.

What Do We Do in Practices?

Good practices do not just happen—they have to be well-planned and well-orchestrated. You must spend some time prior to every practice laying out a schedule and committing it to writing. As the season progresses, you will learn what your team needs to be working on and you can customize your practice schedules accordingly. Remember to keep your practices fun—especially for the younger players. Following are some ideas that can make your practices more fun and productive:

Baseball/Egg Toss: Pair up your players and have the partners stand about a foot apart, facing each other. They begin tossing an egg or a ball back and forth, taking a step backward each time a successful catch occurs. This game works well in teaching the players hand-eye coordination. When the egg or ball is dropped, the two players are out. The last two players standing win baseball cards or some other prize.

Base Pad Race: Line your players up behind home plate. Start the first player running around the bases. When he is halfway down the first base line, start the next player running around the bases. If a player is passed, he has to sit out. This drill is fun, but it also gives you an opportunity to teach the proper techniques to approaching and rounding the bases, and it is a good way to finish a practice. Always have your fastest players line up at the end of the line. Also, use this drill to teach your players to watch the base coaches as they round the bases. Get them used to the basic signals of base coaches: the arm going in a windmill means to keep running, the palms facing the runner means to stop, and the palms facing the ground means to slide.

4-on-4-on-4: Split your team into three teams of four players each. Make sure each team is balanced, and, if your team is old enough to have pitchers, each team has at least one pitcher. Play a live scrimmage with one team batting and the other two teams in the field. Keep score and use a reward for the winning team such as allowing them to be exempt from some conditioning drills.

Error-Free Fielding: With your infielders and outfielders all taking infield positions, have a coach hit ground balls, line drives, and infield pop-ups spread around the infield. The balls should be hit in rapid-fire succession, and the team should keep track of how many balls are fielded for imaginary put outs without errors. Keep track of the most balls caught in a row, and have them try to beat that number. Your team will remember their record, and you can carry this competition on to the next time you conduct this drill. To run a variation of this drill, have a few of your players run the bases as the balls are hit. This tactic creates a more game-like condition and allows your team to get used to having live base runners.

Old-Fashioned Pepper: Place four or five players in a semicircle around a coach. The coach chokes up on a bat and hits bouncers or line drives to the players in the circle. When the player fields the ball he quickly throws it half-speed back to the coach who hits the ball back to that player or another one around the semicircle. You can turn this drill into a game simply by keeping track of the misses—the first player to reach a certain number is out. This game helps players with hand-eye coordination and helps them to keep their eyes on the ball.

Pickle Drill: This drill is sometimes referred to as a rundown drill. Inevitably, your team will catch a player who has overrun his base. In the older age groups, where leadoffs are allowed, the pitcher will catch a base runner too far off the base. Practicing this move is like practicing a dance routine—it needs to be choreographed so that every player knows where to go. Have all the players shout the word *pickle* as loudly as possible, and then run to their spots based on the situation. Use live runners with the goal of being able to either get an out or to force the base runner back to where he started. The shouting of the word *pickle* followed by a smooth choreographed execution tends to intimidate the base runner specifically, and the other team in general.

Pop-Up Drill: Throw or hit pop-up fly balls to your fielders. Early in the season, you might consider using tennis balls and a tennis racket to get your players used to seeing the ball. As a coach, you will find that the racket gives you a bit more control than hitting the ball with a bat, and it is more realistic than throwing pop-ups. The purpose of this drill is to teach them how to catch pop-ups. Make sure that your fielders, especially the infielders, get in the habit of shouting, "I have it" or "It's mine," at the tops of their lungs so there is no question regarding who plans to make the catch. The practice of calling for the fly ball needs to become second nature. Any time during the practice that a player does not call for the fly, point it out to the player. Your entire team will hear this correction, and it will always be on their minds. In addition to making the call, your players need to learn which position has priority when fielding pop-ups. Two rules need to be instilled during this drill: the fielder who is running *in* should take the ball over a fielder who is running *out*, and the fielder who doesn't have to reach across his body should take the ball. By teaching these two principles, your players will learn which teammate is in the best position to make the out.

Bunt in the Buckets: This drill will help your team master that all-important element of the game—the bunt. Place two large plastic trash cans in fair territory down each base line, with the open end pointing toward home plate. The object is to have your players bunt balls into the trash cans. A game can be made by keeping track of how many balls end up in the trash cans. Bunts can be a crucial offensive tool, and they are often overlooked by youth baseball coaches.

Throw Into the Bucket: While you have the trash cans at your practice, use them to help infielders and outfielders develop accuracy in their throwing arms. You will want to move the cans around, but the basic concept is to have your players use them as targets and attempt to throw balls in the cans. This drill is especially helpful for outfielders as they attempt to throw the ball home or to any base. It helps all players develop more accurate arms.

Many other drills can be used during practices—the idea is to be creative and don't get stuck in a routine doing the same thing at every practice. The players and the coaches will get bored, and parents will have to coerce their children into attending your practices.

Make sure your practices are fun, but do not allow the fun to get out of control. Constantly remind them that *you play like you practice*, and that they have to focus on the drills. As the season moves on, they will see the results. Be patient and always do your part in preparing a practice schedule—coaches need to lead by example and work hard with the kids.

Practice Games

No matter how organized you are and how much fun you plan into your practices, they are never as much fun as a real game. Try to schedule a minimum of two pre-season practice games. A good way to insure that you have enough field time is to set up a game with a team that has a practice time adjacent to yours. Bridging two practice times gives you two to three hours, which is plenty of time to play a full game.

In addition to the fun factor, practice games are important to see where you stand with your team and what you need to focus on in future practices. They are also good for the team and the coaches to realize what everyone's roles will be during a game. Do everything just as you would if it was a real game. Steps for managing the team on game days will be further discussed in Chapter 3. Be sure to follow these steps during practice games to get everyone used to the game-day routine. All the rules that apply during a regular game need to be followed, including having your scorekeeper keep the score book exactly as you want it kept in a game. The pre-season games allow you and your scorekeeper to understand each other so that he gives you the information you wish to track in your team stats.

Use signals for bunting, taking, and (if your team is old enough) stealing. The batter needs to be taught to look down the third base line for the signal before he steps in for every pitch. This routine needs to be started in the pre-season games.

Remember to send an announcement (see Chapter 6) home with your players to inform the parents of your practice games, and encourage them to attend. This reminder gets your parents in the habit of supporting the team, and attending the scrimmage games allows them to start learning the players' names and getting to know the other parents. Strong parental involvement is key to a successful season.

Wrap-Up

The team is built on the practice field. Serious practicing creates teams that know what they are supposed to do in game situations. Having fun is important, but goofing off can not be tolerated. Humor keeps practices light and fun, just do not allow it to get out of control. Be organized in your approach to practices, and make sure that your team has enough practice times available. Be consistent and caring in your approach with your players. Repetition in your drills will insure that your team shows up prepared for games. Everyone should come out of the pre-season with an understanding of their particular roles on the team, including players, coaches, and parents. The first game is right around the corner—it's time to hear the umpire cry out, "Play ball!"

Practice Makes Pickles Perfect

Every so often in your coaching experience, you luck out and run into a situation that you can readily use to demonstrate to your team that the time on the practice field really does pay off. In a game, we caught a base runner off the bag, and we found ourselves in a rundown situation. We had covered what to do in rundown or pickle situations several times during our practices, but the way we handled this real-life situation was deplorable. As a result of our execution, my coaches and I decided that we would spend an expanded part of our next practice time on what we refer to as the *pickle drill*.

Countless times we choreographed exactly what each player's role would be in every conceivable situation. We rotated pitchers and fielders so that each boy knew what his responsibility would be, not only in each of these situations but also in every position.

It was monotonous, tedious, and boring—it was all we could do to keep the boys focused on the routine—but, it was exactly what we needed. We tried to have some fun with it, so we had everyone on the team yell, "Pickle" at the tops of their lungs when someone got caught off base. It got to be part of the drill to make sure everyone yelled loudly. We laughed and kept at it for nearly the entire practice.

Here's the good part—the part that allows me to demonstrate the fact that practice does pay off. During our very next game, we caught not one, but three different runners in a pickle, and everyone successfully executed their roles to get the players out. The boys thought it was hilarious that we had spent so much time practicing the pickles, and then we were able to use what we had worked on so soon and so often. Without fail, everyone yelled, "Pickle" at the tops of their lungs and, without a single error, made three clean put outs.

The funniest part for the coaches and parents was to see the expressions on the faces of the other team's players each time our Birds cried out, "Pickle," in unison. That cry alone psyched out the other team, but what was more impressive was the way our boys knew where they needed to go in each scenario to get the out.

They looked more like a well-choreographed dance team than a baseball team, but they were able to relate to the direct correlation between practice time and game execution. They realized that they were much better equipped to handle a pickle situation during a game after the excessive amount of practice doing the drills. The difference was like night and day—practice did pay off.

3

Batter Up! Play Ball!
The First Game Is Here!

*"The way a team plays as a whole determines its success.
You may have the greatest bunch of individual stars in the
world, but if they don't play together,
the club won't be worth a dime."*

—Babe Ruth

You've had the day circled on your calendar since the draft. You've prepared and you've practiced, and now it has finally arrived. The routines you practiced in the pre-season, the drills, and the formation of *team* will all be put to their first test. The players start to arrive and a bit of panic sets in as you realize that they (including your other coaches) are all looking to you for direction. You are the man in charge, the boss, the head coach. This chapter will walk you through how to give your players and coaches the unmistakable impression that you *are* in charge and you *do* know what you are doing. From the pre-game preparation to the end-of-game meeting, the following points represent a step-by-step process to managing game day.

Pre-Game Preparation

Things tend to get crazy rather quickly as your players and coaches arrive at the field. To avoid chaos and confusion, you need to arrive at the field at least 5 to 10 minutes prior to the time you told your team to be there. You should not have anything to do at the field except give your undivided attention to your team. You should come to the field on game day completely prepared. Your batting lineup should be set, your scorebook should be ready, etc. Attempting to make your lineup at the field is asking for trouble. The process of determining your lineup will be discussed in detail in Chapter 5.

Sporting goods stores usually carry four- or five-part lineup sheets (Figure 3-1). These sheets will prove invaluable as they provide copies for your assistant coaches, the dugout coach, the opposing coach, and, if necessary, the umpire. Have your sheet filled out and ready to go. Also, transpose this information into your scorebook. A copy of this form or a pre-purchased lineup clipboard needs to be hung in a prominent place in the dugout (Figure 3-2). The clipboard is convenient since the player names simply slide in and out of the slots, and it is easier to see because it can hang in the dugout. Again, this material needs to be ready prior to your arrival at the field. The preparation at home will allow you to think about your lineup without 12 or 13 players tugging at you.

HIT After HIT
399-BATS
LINE-UP CARD

TEAM _SPARROW RECORDS_ DATE _4/21/2003_

	NO.	PLAYERS	POS		NO.	PLAYERS	POS
1	34	AUSTIN HUFF	CF	12			
SUB				SUB			
2	6	JAKE BEAM	C	13			
SUB				SUB			
3	45	NEAL JOSEPH	SS	14			
SUB				SUB			
4	00	SPENCER HILL	P	15			
SUB				SUB			
5	23	JOHN WEBB	1B	16			
SUB				SUB			
6	21	KEITH GREEN	3B	17			
SUB				SUB			
7	17	BILL PHILLIPS	LF	18			
SUB				SUB			
8	3	MICKY NORRIS	2B				
SUB					NO.	SUBSTITUTES	POS
9	15	NORMAN MILLER	RF		8	PAUL ABRAHAM	
SUB					22	MATT HAINES	
10					14	MATT ROSS	
SUB					5	JOHN KNIGHT	
11							
SUB							

MGR. _____

B&B STAT-MASTER • P.O. BOX 60747 • NASHVILLE, TN 37206

Figure 3-1. Five-part lineup card

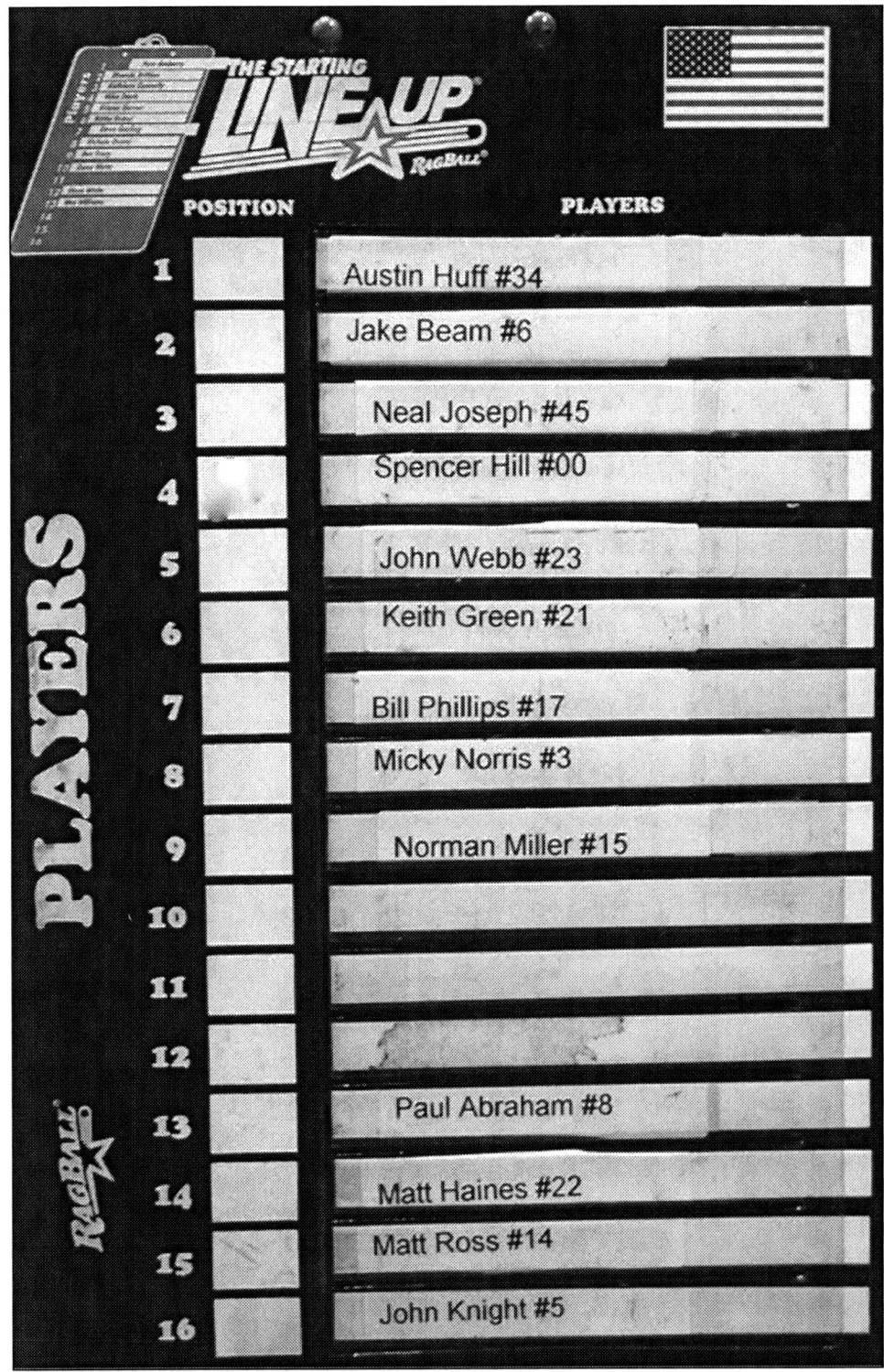

Figure 3-2. Lineup clipboard for offensive batting order

In addition to the batting order, you should have the first and, possibly, second inning defensive lineup prepared. Just like the batting lineup, the defensive lineup needs to be hanging somewhere in the dugout. Erasable whiteboards are designed for this purpose and can be purchased at a local sporting goods store or online (Figure 3-3).

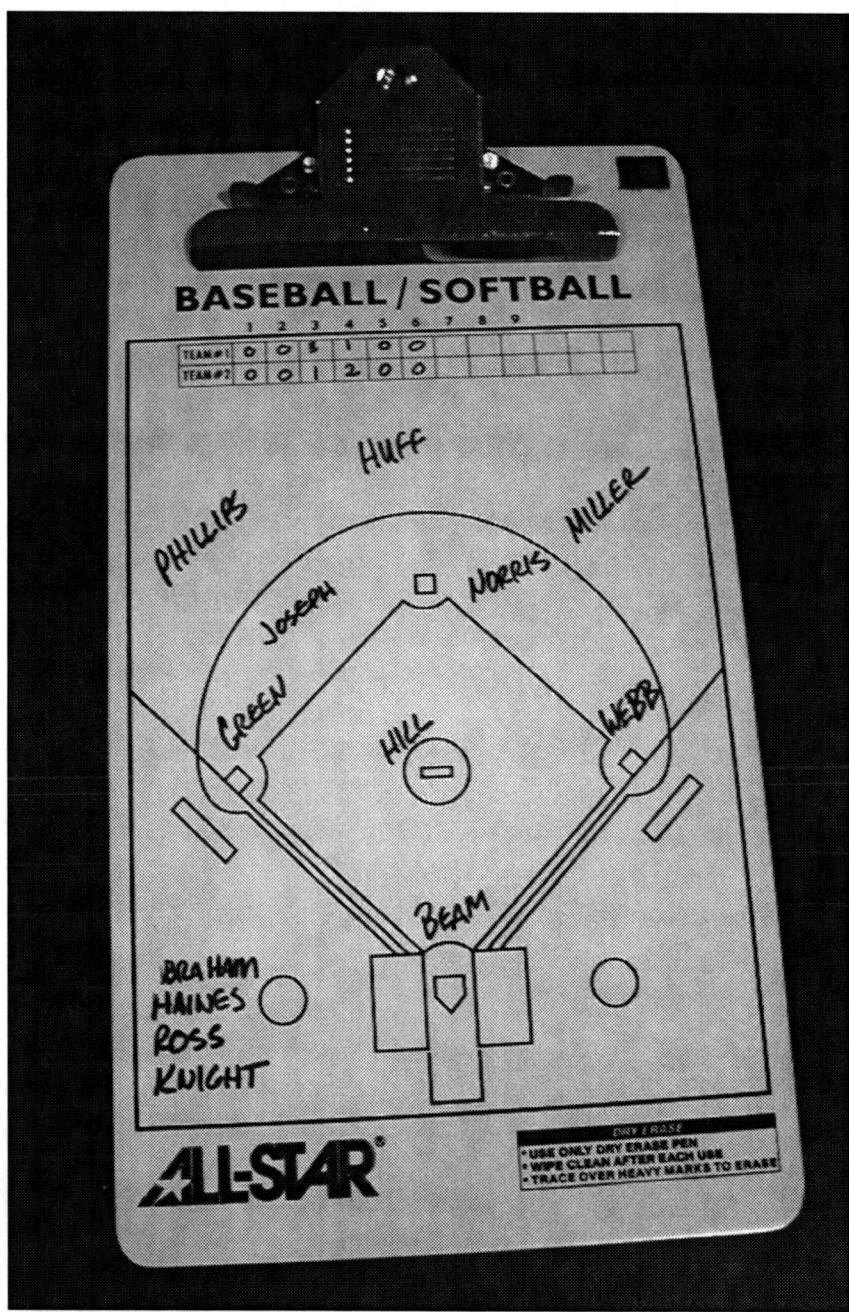

Figure 3-3. Erasable whiteboard for defense

Pre-Game Rituals

You have done all your homework, and now you wait as the players begin to arrive at the field. You will want to decide on a consistent time to have your team arrive at the field before each game—generally, 30 minutes prior to game time works well. The amount time is not important—the consistency is. You do not want to have your parents wondering if they should be there 30 or 45 minutes early. Always allow for the same amount of time for pre-game activities.

As the players arrive, have them grab a ball and a partner and spread down whichever baseline your dugout is on. Have one player stand on or around the foul line and the other in the outfield, approximately 10 yards apart. Your players will tend to edge farther than 10 yards apart as they chase missed balls, and you or another coach will have to constantly rein them in. You not only want them warming their arms up properly, but also you want them playing pitch-and-catch rather than pitch-and-chase. This process should be automatic, as they have been doing this same routine at the practices and pre-season games.

About 20 minutes prior to game time, have them form a circle and have a coach or a player lead the team in stretching exercises. If you select a player to lead, make sure he understands the process. Arms, shoulders, and legs should all be stretched. Jumping jacks and push-ups can also be beneficial and easy for everyone to follow. Place special emphasis on the hamstring muscle as this is highly susceptible to being pulled with the quick starts out of the batting box following a hit. Stretch for 5 to 10 minutes.

Following the stretching time, pull your team together for a pre-game meeting/pep talk. Have the boys take a knee, and then, share with them any information about your opponent that might be helpful—offensively or defensively. Read the starting lineup and starting positions, and, if your team is old enough, review the signs that your third-base coach will use to communicate to the base runners and batters. If you choose to do so, this meeting is a great opportunity to pray with your team that they would play with sportsmanship and that no injuries would occur to either team.

At some point during warm-ups, you should exchange lineup cards with the opposing coach and coordinate which team will take the field first for infield practice. Normally, the home team takes the field last so they can remain in the field for the start of the game—the home team gets the advantage of batting last. However, there may be extenuating circumstances that would warrant a switch in tradition.

Following the prayer and just prior to taking the field for infield practice, have all the players gather close and put their hands in the center of a circle for a huddle-breaking cheer such as, *"Team* on three…one, two, three…*team!"* Whatever word you choose to use for the cheer, be consistent. It could be the name of your mascot, your sponsor, or whatever word your team prefers. The word is not important—enthusiasm is. The cheer should be designed to pull your team together and spark some pre-game excitement. The louder the cheer is shouted, the better. You want to let your opponent hear you and know your boys are fired up.

Following the breakdown, have your team take the field. Establish a rule that no one on your team ever *walks* onto the field—everyone *runs* on and off the field. Watch winning teams and notice how they hustle. The no-walking-onto-the-field rule is important to demonstrate the character of your team. However, your pitcher should be exempt from this rule as pitchers need to conserve energy whenever possible.

Your pre-game infield practice should involve a coach hitting grounders around the horn and making plays to first. Some coaches practice turning two outs by going to second base and then to first. This maneuver may be too advanced for the younger age groups—how often have you seen a double play turned in the early age groups— Regardless of your philosophy on this point, you should practice going to second with a throw to get the lead runner. On the final round, have the players come home with their throws.

While one coach is hitting to the infielders, another coach should hit fly balls to the starting outfielders and the nonstarting players. Keep order to this drill by not having more than one player going for a fly ball, which is an accident waiting to happen. Only one player should be up at a time, and everyone should be aware of whose turn it is. It's helpful to have one of the nonstarting players catch for each coach. The starting pitcher and catcher should be warming up away from the action.

Now, you've done all your homework, the pre-game rituals (including infield and outfield practices) are complete, the parents are in the stands, and your players are ready to play a real game. It's time to get started and enjoy the great game of baseball.

During the Game

Order in the dugout and discipline on the field during the game are both keys to success. Teach the players what the dugout rules are and enforce them (Figure 3-4). If your team is young enough to have a dugout coach, have that person in the dugout, helping to maintain order. Teach your players that once they choose where they will sit on the bench, they need to keep the same seat throughout the game. This sounds harsh, but it makes everyone's life easier when young players are not fighting for their seats on the bench. Another difficult thing for young players to do is to keep track of their hats and gloves. Inevitably, little Johnny is late getting to the field because one of those two key items is nowhere to be found. To avoid this scenario in the dugout, teach your coaches and players that, when they come into the dugout, they should place their hats and gloves directly under their "assigned" seat for that particular game.

ABC
Records & Publishing

Dugout Rules and Behavior

◊ Sit in the same spot on the bench from inning to inning.

◊ Your hat (if it's not on your head) and glove should always be under the seat where you are sitting.

◊ Never climb on the fence.

◊ Cheer for your teammates!

◊ Listen to the dugout coach at all times.

◊ When you're on deck, warm up on the third-base side when a right-handed hitter is batting, and on the first-base side when a left-handed hitter is batting.

◊ Pick up any trash you see and put it in the proper container—keep the dugout neat.

◊ Never ignore the game when you're in the dugout.

Figure 3-4. Dugout rules

The other key responsibility of your dugout coach is to insure that everyone is aware of the batting order (i.e., who is up to bat next, who is on deck, and who is in the hole (third up), etc.). Even when you team outgrows the need for a designated dugout coach, always assign the batting order responsibility to one of your assistants.

You or an assistant coach must constantly be assigning defensive positions for future innings. Remember as you rotate players in and out (assuming your league allows for free substitution rather than following official baseball substitution rules, in which a player cannot come back in once he leaves a game), the parents are there to see their children play—not just sit the bench. If your league does not have specific rules regarding playing time, make sure that all your players see time in the field. To help manage playing time, use the form provided in the roster template on the companion CD-ROM (Figure 3-5). The initials (A, PO, and E for assists, putouts, and errors) in the right-hand columns will assist you in the creation of fielding stats, and they will be explained more in Chapter 5. These records are best kept in a binder so you have a detailed history of the number of defensive innings each player played. Do not post this form in the dugout, but have an assistant or a player transfer the information for each upcoming inning onto the whiteboard throughout the game. Players will learn to look at the board each inning before taking the field, and they won't be asking questions as your team takes the field.

ABC
Records & Publishing

VS. _____

DEFENSIVE LINEUP (NOT BATTING ORDER)

NAME	#	INNING							A	PO	E
		1	2	3	4	5	6	7			
Paul Abraham	8										
Jake Beam	6										
Keith Green	21										
Spencer Hill	0										
Austin Huff	34										
Matt Haines	22										
Neal Joseph	45										
John Knight	5										
Norman Miller	15										
Micky Norris	3										
Bill Phillips	17										
Matt Ross	14										
John Webb	23										

Figure 3-5. Defensive lineup form

These tips simply add to smooth flow and limit the confusion that generally permeates an unorganized coach's dugout between innings. The coach who is managing the dugout must make sure that the players are where they are supposed to be. It is obvious where the batter and the player on deck should be. The player in the hole (third up) and the player in the deep hole (fourth up) should be in an area designated for soft toss into a fence or, preferably, a hitting net. Doing so gives the hitters additional time to warm up and get used to "seeing" the baseball. This procedure is most important in the early innings but should be maintained throughout the game to keep your hitters sharp.

Following each inning as your team comes in from the field, have them huddle outside the dugout. All players should be included in this mini-meeting, including the players who were sitting on the bench that inning. Use this time to critique your team's play. However, avoid singling out a particular player's performance. This motivational technique will be discussed in more detail in Chapter 4.

Throughout the game, you and your assistant coaches must make sure order is maintained in the dugout and your players are disciplined on the field. Make sure all players are paying attention to the game. Randomly and periodically ask players what the score is, how many outs there are, what inning it is, or some other question pertinent to the game. This tactic helps to keep your guys into the game.

Your assistant coaches, and especially you as the head coach, must set an example for the players and the parents. Never lose your temper with an umpire or another coach. Limit the number of discussions that you have with the umpires. Monitor your assistants and players carefully. Do not tolerate trash talking, bad mouthing, foul language, or arguing calls with umpires by anyone. Remember, no one coaches but the coaches, and no one discusses questionable calls with the umpires but you—the head coach. These points may seem insignificant, but they go a long way in distinguishing your team as one that handles itself with character and class. To assist you with the parents and to remind you and your coaches of the responsibilities of being coaches, it is a good idea to give everyone a copy of the handouts "Parents' Code of Ethics" and "Coaches' Code of Ethics" (Figures 3-6 and 3-7).

Following the final out—win or lose—make sure your players line up to shake hands with the other team. Try to shake the umpires' hands, and make it a point to congratulate or encourage the other coaches. It is your responsibility to make sure these rituals takes place. And now that you have finished the game and your team has won or lost, it's time to move to the postgame activities.

ABC
Records & Publishing

Parents' Code of Ethics

◊ I will encourage good sportsmanship by demonstrating positive support for all players, coaches, and officials at every game, practice, or other youth sports event.

◊ I will place the emotional and physical well-being of my child ahead of a personal desire to win.

◊ I will insist that my child play in a safe and healthy environment.

◊ I will support coaches and officials working with my child, in order to encourage a positive and enjoyable experience for all.

◊ I will demand a sports environment for my child that is free of drugs, tobacco, and alcohol, and will refrain from their use at all youth sports events.

◊ I will remember that the game is for youth-not for adults.

◊ I will do my very best to make youth sports fun for my child.

◊ I will ask my child to treat other players, coaches, fans, and officials with respect, regardless of race, sex, creed, or ability.

◊ I promise to help my child enjoy the youth sports experience by doing whatever I can, such as being a respectful fan, assisting with coaching, or providing transportation.

◊ I will require that my child's coach be trained in the responsibilities of being a youth sports coach, and the coach upholds the Coaches' Code of Ethics.

©National Alliance for Youth Sports

Figure 3-6. Parents' code of ethics

ABC
Records & Publishing

Coaches' Code of Ethics

◊ I will place the emotional and physical well-being of my players ahead of a personal desire to win.

◊ I will treat each player as an individual, remembering the large range of emotional and physical development for the same age group.

◊ I will do my best to provide a safe playing situation for my players.

◊ I will promise to review and practice the basic first aid principles needed to treat injuries of players.

◊ I will do my best to organize practices that are fun and challenging for all my players.

◊ I will lead by example in demonstrating fair play and sportsmanship to all my players.

◊ I will be knowledgeable in the rules of each sport that I coach and I will teach these rules to my players.

◊ I will use those coaching techniques appropriate for each of the skills that I teach.

◊ I will remember that I am a youth sports coach and that the game is for children and not adults.

©National Alliance for Youth Sports

Figure 3-7. Coaches' code of ethics

Postgame

Before your players leave the dugout after the game, make sure that they do three things: pack up their equipment—make sure they have *everything*, pick up any trash to leave the dugout clean for the next team, and make sure that everyone knows where the postgame meeting is going to be held. Win or lose, it's important to gather your team to have one last talk before releasing them back to their parents. Invite the parents to gather around to hear what you have to say—it makes them feel like a part of the team.

Giving away game balls is a great form of encouragement and should be done at the postgame meeting. Packs or individual baseball cards can also be awarded for specific plays or attitudes that you would like to recognize. More about game balls and card rewards can be found in Chapter 4.

Use the time during the postgame meeting to hand out players' stats (see Chapter 5) and to make any announcements that need to be made. If you need parental feedback on any issues, this meeting is a good time to ask for that. Conclude the meeting by having the team huddle together, put their hands in, and break it down for one last cheer. The last thing you should say after the breakdown is when and where the team will get together next.

The parent who signed up for snacks can now give the snacks to the players—do try and delay the snacks until after the meeting. Eating during the postgame meeting can be a distraction with the young age groups. It is important to maintain control of your team at all times. In fact, the three most important things to remember when coaching a team are discipline, discipline, and discipline. Chapter 4 discusses how to have a disciplined team and still maintain a fun environment where your players will flourish.

Wrap-Up

You have completed your first game. Your preparation in the pre-season and immediately prior to your game has paid off, and you see positive signs of encouragement as your players begin to mold into a team. During the day, you have noted things that both your team and your coaches (perhaps even your parents) and you need to work on during future practices or coaches meetings. Don't expect to have everything run as smoothly as you would like after your first game, but now you have a formula to follow. Remember the seven Ps of teambuilding and press on. As you follow the plans in this book, you will see that you are setting yourself apart from the vast majority of volunteer coaches. Remember, persistence, patience, and, above all, principle as you move forward.

Now that you have a general framework on which to build your team—a skeleton, so to speak—the next few chapters will give you some meat to put on the bones. Chapter 4 will show you how to get the most out of your players.

Teaching More Than Baseball

Life happens on the ballfield. This point was made quite clear to me early on in my years of coaching youth baseball. Our team, the Sparrow Records Birds, was sponsored by a Christian music company headquartered in our town. I was an executive with the company, so a baseball team sponsorship was a natural. As a result of this connection and my own personal faith, a team prayer was a part of our pre-game meeting just prior to us taking the field or preparing for our first at bat.

I was often the one who led the prayer time, but to allow the players to see and hear other adults praying, I would share the responsibility with my assistant coaches. Rarely would we have a player ask if he could pray. At one of our meetings prior to a critical game, I had gone through the starting lineup and given the team some motivational thoughts. I was prepared to ask the boys to remove their hats to lead them in the pre-game prayer.

The boys knew the routine, and just as I was going for my hat, a mild-mannered, 10-year-old voice spoke up and said, "Coach Rod, would it be ok if I prayed tonight?" Of course, I said yes, and young Bill proceeded to talk with God—allowing us to eavesdrop on his conversation.

Bill explained to God, and the rest of his team, that his Pap was very ill and he was going to be operated on the next day in a hospital far away in Pennsylvania. It was an innocent and sincere plea for God to spare his Pap and not take him to heaven just yet, as he would miss him terribly. He told us all how much he loved his Pap, and he asked for comfort for his Dad who was at his Pap's bedside. The prayer was very mature for a 10-year-old and very moving. Having been through many serious illnesses with my father, my son and I were both touched by young Bill's concerns and the anxiety he was feeling.

At the "Amen," the coaches and I were brushing away tears as we raised our heads. Not quite sure what to say next, I was silent until one of the players spoke up and said, "Okay guys, we're going to win this game for Bill's grandfather!" This suggestion was embraced by all the Birds. Bill loved the idea and appreciated the gesture.

At this point in our meetings, we would usually put our hands together in a circle and break it down with a cheer, "*Birds* on three…one, two, three…*Birds!*" As we all put our hands in the center of the circle, I changed the word *Birds* to *Pap*. The boys immediately got it and yelled, "Pap," louder than any breakdown of the season to that point.

The story has a happy ending because Pap made it through his surgery with flying colors. That simple request of a frightened young man drew that year's team much closer to each other. We won the game that night for Bill's Pap and, better yet, his Pap was able to attend one of our year-end tournament games to thank the Birds personally for their prayers.

4

That a Boy!
Motivational Coaching

*"Unless you try to do something you have never mastered,
you will never grow."*

—Scott Jones
Former Head Volleyball Coach
Trevecca Nazarene University

*"A coach is someone who always makes you do what you don't
want to do, so you can be who you've always wanted to be."*

—Unknown

A vital component in formulating a successful team and a rewarding season is motivation. A common thread that runs through great coaches—throughout all sports—is the ability to get the most out of their players. For example, year after year, John Wooden, head coach of the UCLA basketball team from 1964-1975, fielded one strong team after another and won an unprecedented 10 NCAA titles in his 12-year tenure. Granted, the reputation of the program and his track record contributed to his strong recruiting classes year after year, but he relied on getting the most out of all of his players, while he focused his practices on fundamentals. He consistently played deep into his bench based on the idea that no one player is more important than the team. John Wooden was a world-class motivator and teambuilder.

The old cliché *you catch more flies with honey than vinegar* also holds true in coaching. The gruff coach who belittles, humiliates, and browbeats his players does not work in today's world. The model of the modern, successful coach is one of an organized encourager and teacher. This chapter will take you through opportunities for motivation and give you some ideas that you may wish to incorporate into your program.

Motivation During Practices

As discussed in Chapter 2, practices need to be designed to improve your team's abilities. As a coach, you will have more opportunities to motivate during practices than you will during games. Be purposeful in your interactions with your team during practices. Walk around and talk with your players during periods of idle time. No matter how well you plan your practices, you will have idle time for some players, some of the time. Part of your practice schedule should include times for you and your assistant coaches to walk around and talk to individual players. The topics you discuss should range from specific baseball skills to personal issues. Learn what's going on in the lives of your players when they are away from the ballfield.

It will be interesting what you hear and discover. Some players will have parents who are separating or family members who are ill, and some may be struggling at school, etc. As you listen, you are building a relationship and trust. As a coach, you are not necessarily trained to be a counselor, so do not attempt to play that role. However, by showing an interest in their lives outside of baseball, you become more credible. Your players think, *Hey, this guy really cares about me, maybe I should respect him and listen to what he has to tell me*. Steven Covey in his hugely successful book, *The 7 Habits of Highly Effective People*, discusses the concept of emotional bank accounts. By showing care and concern for your players outside the world of baseball, you are making "deposits" into their emotional bank accounts. These deposits, made throughout the season, afford you the opportunity to make withdrawals when you need them for the sake of the team or other players later on. Players who feel an emotional connection are more apt to give the team their all.

Practice times also give you chances to point out things that are being done well, while you are correcting your players' faults and problems. Coaches who only point out the negative and neglect the "attaboys," often have dissatisfied players and, consequently, parents as the season drags on. Always look for opportunities to give compliments along with corrections.

During your practices, do not hesitate to stop a drill or a play to have a teaching moment. If appropriate and important enough, call your entire team together to replay and correct something that you observed. Be careful not to embarrass anyone, but often, these observations can be helpful to the entire team. Handled correctly, these moments can be motivating as well as educational.

Practices need to be fun, but never forget the opportunities to motivate and build *team*. Never allow fun to get in the way of learning. Know your players, and know what areas they are strong in and what areas they are deficient in. Work on the deficiencies and emphasize the strengths. Never cast off a weaker player as a "no-way" player—you can always find some positive aspect about a player to praise. As a coach, your words can be harsh and cutting or positive and affirming. Be aware of this concept as you interact with your team, and always attempt to build your players' confidence.

Motivation During Games

Like in practice, it is inevitable that many good and bad things will happen during your games. You will likely have days when it seems like everything is going poorly, but if you look hard enough, you can find reasons to celebrate or congratulate. Never pass up the good times—especially the ones for players who do not often have something to celebrate. Don't rely on your memory alone to recall special moments or plays. Keep a clipboard or a small notebook to write on during games. Your memory may fail and you could end up forgetting to recognize little Johnny's only caught fly ball for the season. Write these things down somewhere or you may regret it later.

As discussed in Chapter 3, as your players come in from the field, always conduct a brief meeting outside of the dugout. This gathering is a good opportunity to recap the defensive side of the inning and refocus your team on their upcoming at bat. The players who sat on the bench that inning may need to be reminded to join their teammates, but make sure everyone huddles up for the meeting—this exercise is important to keep the team unified. During this time, point out any great defensive plays by using the name(s) of the player(s) involved, and explain to the other players why it was such a good play. If the team makes a mistake or you see something that needs to be corrected for more than one player, go ahead and point that out in these meetings. Encourage your pitcher after every inning. Highlight the good things he did and restore his confidence following an inning where the opposing players may have tallied up a lot of hits.

It is best not to correct an individual player in front of the entire team. Pull a player aside to talk with him separately about any mistakes he may have made. Depending upon the relationship, you may feel comfortable having a bit of fun at the expense of one of your better players who may have pulled a bonehead move. As the season progresses, you will know which players can handle having fun being poked at them. This approach often lightens the mood of your team and helps them to feel loose and relaxed.

Keeping your team focused becomes easier as your players get older. In the younger age groups, you are constantly reminding the players not to play in the dirt and not to misplace their hats and gloves in the dugout. The older they get, the more motivational you can be and the more detailed you can get in teaching the finer points of the game. If you sense that your team is flat or just not paying attention, have them put their hands in and break it down (e.g., *Team* (or whatever word you choose) on three…one, two, three…*team!*) It's best to find a player-leader among your players, and ask him to serve as the "cheerleader" for the breakdown when necessary. Be careful not to overuse this tactic or it will lose its ability to rally your team.

These meetings are also a good time to talk about what your team needs to do to win the game. Encourage your hitters and keep track of any team records that you have a chance to break. Above all, keep your team focused on the task at hand. And remember, all of these points need to be crammed into a 30- to 45-second window between innings. So, think about what you want to communicate based on how the inning has gone. Again, it's good to take notes during the game—do not rely on your memory alone.

If your league has conducted a fair draft, you should not notice much disparity in the talent that each team puts on the field. Sometimes, the difference will be in how well you and the other coaches motivate your team. Enthusiastic teams follow a motivated, enthusiastic leader. Be animated and excited about your coaching experience—it will truly rub off on your team. Likewise, a tired, boring coach will be reflected in the spirit and attitude of his team. Go to the ballpark and observe. And then, notice which of the two extremes usually ends up with the *W*. An enthusiastic team trumps a deadbeat team, and enthusiastic teams also trump equally-talented teams.

You and your assistant coach will likely act as the base coaches. When the players reach your base, celebrate those little victories—especially with the players who do not reach the bases regularly. No matter the age, players need to be reminded of the basics about base running every time they reach first base. Remind them to pay attention, watch for line drives, take a few steps off the bag, and watch when fly balls are hit. They also need to be reminded to watch and listen to their base coaches as they run the bases, They need to pick up on the signs so they will know what the batter is doing and to see if the steal is on for them. Constantly remind your players of the necessity of paying attention to the base coaches.

Psychology of Winners

Many of the things you do to motivate your team can serve to intimidate your opponents. For instance, have a rule that only the pitcher is allowed to walk on or off the field. Every other player must run to his position. This rule also applies during your pre-game warm-ups. The hard-and-fast rule is that no one, except the pitcher, walks onto the field. Carry this rule to your batters. *Hustle* is the key. If you have a player who draws a walk, they need to be taught to run to first base. Teams (especially younger age groups) do not expect this move, and your player will often end up on second base. The excitement created by a batter who runs when he is walked can cause confusion for the opposing players. When that fourth ball is pitched, the catcher may not be able to get a good handle on it. Then, when he sees your player running down the baseline, he often gets excited trying to scoop the ball up, and in the excitement, he may overthrow the ball. The bottom line is that your batter turns a base on balls into a double, and the other team realizes that your team means business. When opponents see how your players hustle, they start to think that your team is a serious contender. It's a simple concept, but it's true and it works.

In addition to always hustling, your team needs to *look* like a team. Shirttails should be tucked in, hats should be on straight, and uniforms should always be matching. As the season progresses, your players may start to show up with the wrong hats, socks or belts that are the wrong color, etc. Do not allow this practice to continue. You should either provide extra uniform pieces or let the parents know where they can be purchased. Your team needs to always look like they mean business—it's part of the psychology of the game.

Postgame Motivation

As discussed in Chapter 3, your last words to the players before sending them off with their parents are said during the time that you huddle with them following the game. Postgame meetings have a much better feel to them following a victory. However, win or lose, have the meeting. Celebrate your victories, and use losses as opportunities to teach lessons. Remember to clearly state where the meeting will take place, and invite your parents to gather around.

To keep their attention, have your players take a knee for the meeting. It's easier for them to stay focused if they are resting on a knee rather than sprawling out on the grass. If snacks are a part of your postgame ritual, ask the parent in charge of snacks that day to hold off distributing them until after the meeting to keep distractions to a minimum.

As discussed in the previous chapter, use a game ball to highlight the performance of a single player. Keep careful records of who you award game balls to—your players and their parents will definitely watch who gets the coveted acknowledgment. Be diligent with your record keeping. Certain software packages, such as TurboStats, which is recommended in this book, allow the user to customize fields. This topic will be discussed more in Chapter 5. However you choose to keep track of your stats, make sure a player is not awarded a second game ball before every player on the team has earned at least one ball. As you move throughout your season, you will recognize certain players who will have numerous opportunities that would be considered game-ball worthy, as well as the players that you may have to search to find something worth rewarding. Early in the season, if a weaker player does something worth mentioning, you are wise not to pass up that opportunity. You may not get another chance, and it is awkward to make up a reason for giving the game ball such as, "Little Johnny gets the game ball today for really hustling to his right field position." This type of patronizing award doesn't make anyone feel good. Maybe Johnny had a putout, a stolen base, or even a hit in a previous game that you passed up for a more exciting play. Learn your game ball challenges, and make sure your coaches are aware of them so you can all be on the lookout for the little things.

Giving out baseball cards (packs or individual cards) is a good way to recognize anyone who may have contributed in the game but would not be getting a game ball, either because they had already earned one or another player was more deserving. Another option to consider is that your team sponsor may be able to contribute some kind of reward for your cause. For example, if your team is sponsored by a food establishment, they may be happy to provide free burger coupons or something of this nature. Believe it or not, you will need to keep track of these mini-awards as well. Fairness and equal treatment fosters team development. You will have your stars, but try not to build them up too much. Their heads could swell, and then resentment may grow and divide your team.

Have fun during this time, especially when you win. If a player does something goofy—and he has the right kind of personality—have fun with him. Laughter is always a good thing as you develop your team. In the event of a loss, try to find something that your team can take away from the experience. Focus on team efforts. Be aware of the player who was the last out in a close game or who booted a ground ball that resulted in your team losing. Those players need to be shored up. Younger kids can be insensitive and downright mean in those situations. If you hear other players making comments about those kinds of plays, step in and do not allow them to continue. Stress that other bad plays were made that led to the loss and the unfortunate player only committed the last out or the final error. These kinds of little issues can destroy team spirit and divide your team. Break it down with a cheer and remind your players and parents when and where the team will meet next.

Motivation Off the Field

It is important to plan some nonbaseball-related activities for your team. These events are especially important during the pre-season. An excellent teambuilding exercise is to plan a sleepover. The most difficult aspect of planning this event is to find parents who are brave enough to have 12 young men spend the night in their home. Make the plea, or if you have a team mom/dad, delegate the responsibility to them to ask the parents to volunteer for this event. The most important outcome of this type of gathering will be that your players will get to know each other much better, and a unified team will begin to take shape.

Creating unity is your major goal, but it is also a good time to draw upon some of the classic sports films to watch as a group: *Remember the Titans, Hoosiers, The*

Mighty Ducks, Rudy, Facing the Giants, or even *The Bad News Bears* (the original—not the 2006 remake). Plenty of other movies are out there that are examples of a group of players who start out with no chance at all of winning and then become champions. The sleepover experience gives you some common ground and a foundation to begin your teambuilding.

Make the sleepover a priority, but plan other activities as well such as playing laser tag, going out to the movies (especially if there is a new and appropriate sports film in the theaters), or just having an evening at a local pizza parlor following a game or practice. Any of these activities is good, but the pizza gathering is particularly beneficial since it will also involve the parents. As important as it is for your players to get to know each other, it is equally important to purposely plan events where your parents will meet and get to know each other. If your parents get acquainted and enjoy each other's company, they are more apt to attend the games.

All of these nonbaseball-related events will culminate with your end-of-the-year party. Chapter 7 discusses this event in much more detail. Never limit your motivational ideas or teambuilding exercises to the ballfield—great opportunities exist off the field.

Wrap-Up

Always keep in mind that the "little" things identified in this chapter will clearly separate you and your team from the rest of the pack. Your positive, energetic approach will spread to your coaching staff, your players, and even the parents. Be positive and handle your corrections carefully.

Find a way to positively recognize your weaker players and reward their performance. Likewise, be careful not to overcompliment and overpraise your stronger players, which can lead to hard feelings among teammates. Instill a psychology of winning in everything that you do—down to the color of socks your players wear. Hustle is the key, and your entire team must look like ball players throughout the entire season.

Create an environment of family for your team. Plan nonbaseball-related events and invite the parents to participate. As your parents get to know each other, they will have more of a reason to attend your games. Just as hustling and maintaining team appearance attracts the attention of the opposing team, a loud, supportive group of parents also gets their attention.

As you coach and observe other teams, it will become obvious that the ideas presented in this chapter are not widely used. Consequently, they can make a big difference in your team's performance and separate your team from the rest of the teams in your league.

SSSH! Sleeping Bats

One particular "between-innings" meeting made a significant difference in the outcome of the game we were playing. Our team, the Sparrow Birds, was hopelessly behind. After having the opposing hitters pound our pitchers, one after another, our boys were getting discouraged. This situation was aggravated by untimely errors (as if there is a good time for errors) in the field and the inability of our batters to reach first base.

The score was 12-0, and we were about to bat in the bottom of the fourth inning. It was now or never since a lead of 10 runs or more at the end of four innings brought the game to a close under the league's mercy rule.

I gathered a dejected group of Birds together for our usual between-innings meeting, and holding a finger up to my mouth, I simply said, "Sssh!" Confusion ensued as the boys looked around at each other and wondered if Coach Rod had lost it.

Again, I repeated "Sssh," and added, "Be quiet." After an awkward silence, I told them that their bats were asleep in the dugout, and I didn't want to wake them. They got the joke, laughter erupted, and the edge of tension was removed. They proceeded to score nine runs in that at bat and four runs in the bottom of the next inning to win the game as the time limit expired.

Sometimes, teams get into ruts and everything seems to go wrong. The Birds remembered this incident for the rest of that season, and the idea of waking our bats became another rally cry. As the coach, not only can you change the course of a game, it's your responsibility to do so.

I've seen many a coach throw in the towel when they were down in a 12-0 deficit. The sleeping bats story is proof that the tide can be turned. Be creative and relieve the pressure. When teams try too hard not to commit errors, they will inevitably commit more. Likewise, when players try too hard to hit the ball, they will be tense, uptight, and uncomfortable in the batter's box.

Relieving the pressure frees your players to have fun and enjoy the game. The players who were on the "sleeping bats" comeback team can easily recall the details of that game six years later.

The Hangnail Incident

Sometimes, motivational opportunities present themselves quite by accident, which is exactly what happened one year when the Birds were all young teens. As can happen with volunteers, sometimes, due to time commitments or other circumstances, coaches have to step aside and become spectators. This scenario is how I was able to draft Frankie. Frankie's father had coached his teams for years, and he had to step aside. I had competed against Frankie's teams for years and had a great relationship with his father. I had always admired Frankie's competitive spirit.

As first base coach, I would often strike up conversations with our opponent's first baseman, which had been Frankie's position most of the time. He had a great personality and sense of humor, so I looked forward to our games against his team, and I was always pleased to see his smiling face take his normal position at first base. As soon as I saw that he was available to draft, I jumped at the chance to have him become a part of our team.

What I haven't shared to this point is the fact that Frankie had a birth defect, which left him with a fully-developed left hand but merely a small stub at the end of his right forearm. He was so adept at fielding, flipping the ball into the air, and grabbing it with his good hand that most people never even noticed the transition. At bat, his deformed hand pushed the bat through the strike zone, and again, most observers never noticed. He always maintained a high batting average and batted at the top of his team's order. He was also a solid pitcher. He was the complete package and very coachable—every coach's dream.

He was also an inspiration to me, the other players, and the coaches. I'll never forget a particular situation in one of our postseason games. We were scheduled to play a double header on a very hot Saturday afternoon. During the first game, my second baseman, Will, sustained a nasty injury when a ground ball took a bad hop and caught the little fingernail on his throwing hand and bent it back. It was a painful annoyance, but it created a situation that we have had many laughs about over the years.

Let me set the scene for the humor and motivation in this situation. The team was standing in a semicircle talking prior to our formal warm-ups. Will was bemoaning about how much his finger hurt and telling me he didn't know if he could play in game two. Standing next to Will was Frankie with his glove resting on his stub of a hand. I said, "Will, you're telling me you can't play due to a hangnail (downplaying the severity of his injury for affect) when Frankie goes out there for every game and plays with only one hand?"

Frankie joined in the fun and Will was shamed into toughing it up and playing in the second game of the double header. We did move him to an outfield position since the injury did impact his throwing accuracy. This situation was humorous, but the fact was that Frankie had overcome a childhood handicap and competed at the all-star level despite his birth defect. He demonstrated a life lesson for all of us—one that I have referenced countless times in my business management career.

My presentation of Frankie's award at the end of the season party was an emotional one. It was the first time in all my years of coaching that I had to regain my composure before I could continue honoring the boy who overachieved and maintained a positive attitude despite his physical condition.

5

Keeping Good Stats— It's All in the Numbers

"Slump? I ain't in no slump. I just ain't hittin'."

—Yogi Berra

In volunteer baseball coaching, as in anything in life, you must be able to measure results. Whether you are the CEO of a multi-million dollar company or you run a small business out of your garage, you need to know certain key numbers concerning your company. Great CEOs at some of the nation's top companies learned early in their careers that their organizations run more efficiently if they share key numbers and goals with their entire staff.

When traveling, you need a map to find the way to your destination. Along the way, you check the odometer in your car and the mile markers along the road to track mileage and to let you know how far you have progressed on your trip. The same idea holds true with coaching. Just like managing a company or completing a trip—numbers and measurements are critical to your team's success.

Coaching baseball requires that you know and understand your team's strengths and weaknesses, and the only way to assess these areas is to keep good records of your players' goals and overall team goals. Statistics are vital to a team's success, and they are often overlooked when coaching the younger age groups. Top coaches, just like CEOs, know where they are at in relation to their plans. Utilizing stats, from your first year as a volunteer coach, will place you in a small group of dedicated and successful coaches.

Tracking Team Performance

As you observe your opponents, the striking thing that you will notice is that some of the worst teams often use the same batting lineup every time your team faces them. Your lineup should be adjusted for every game. Baseball is a streaky game where at any given point in your season, you may have some players with hot bats and others in the midst of horrible slumps. The only way that you, as the coach, have to track these streaks is to carefully monitor your statistics.

The feedback that using statistics provides to you and your staff will be invaluable. And when everyone, including the parents, is aware that your lineup is created based on statistics, it takes a lot of pressure off of you to explain why little Johnny is batting last. But, equally important, the feedback is beneficial to your players because knowing that the batting order is determined by statistics will help motivate them (and their parents) to spend extra time outside of practice on batting skills to move up in the order.

In addition, even though you should never share a player's individual stats with other players, the players do share voluntarily with each other, and peer pressure tends to raise the bar. An informal competition begins to develop, which motivates your players and improves the team's overall performance at the plate.

Record-Keeping Methods

The process of record-keeping is time consuming and requires a coach who purposefully takes the time to make his team better. The question pops up for a new coach, "How do I do this?" The answer is that it is not an easy task—every method available requires a committed coach. However, the time spent in this off-the-field activity will pay guaranteed dividends in your win column.

The answer to the "how to" part of the question runs the gamut from taking a manual calculation with a sheet of paper and a calculator to using a sophisticated software package designed to make this record-keeping activity much easier. The software packages offer various reporting outputs that allow you to keep your team, coaching staff, and players informed of how your team is doing statistically. The report generation and feedback is much more laborious with the pen-and-paper method.

If you are not skilled with the computer, you will likely be able to find a parent who will volunteer for this job. If you take this approach, the ideal person may be the one who has volunteered to keep your score book. At any rate, the monitoring of your team's stats will be a major differentiator for your team.

The author recommends a program created by TurboStats, a company that specializes in software to track statistics in a number of different sports. To find out more about this company or for ordering information, visit their website: www.turbostats.com. You can download a trial version of the software from the website. The trial program allows you to enter and keep track of six complete games before it locks up. A call to the company and a credit card number will unlock the software and allow you to track as many seasons and teams as you wish. Other brands of software are available, but TurboStats is a proven program that has been around for a number of years. TurboStats also offers a PalmPilot version of the baseball stats program—that trial program can also be downloaded from the TurboStats website.

Whichever program you decide on will be a tremendous improvement over any manual attempt. Better than manual but not as good as a specially-designed program, is the creation of a spreadsheet that attempts to automate much of the manual process. However, even in its best form, it will still fall short of the canned programs. A Microsoft® Excel® or other spreadsheet will be cheaper than using a software package, but it is not nearly as efficient.

Getting Started

The bulk of the material in this chapter is based on the assumption that a canned program, specifically TurboStats, is being utilized. However, the techniques and suggestions can be adapted to whatever method you use to track your statistics. Again, the method is not as important as the fact that you recognize the necessity to track your team's key numbers.

First, enter your players' names and uniform numbers into the program. Most programs will also give you the option to enter addresses, phone numbers, email addresses, etc., which allows you to generate rosters for the parents. However, an Excel spreadsheet can sometimes be more efficient than the stat tracking program for managing certain aspects of your team. The roster will be discussed in Chapter 6.

After your players' names and uniform numbers have safely been saved on your computer's hard drive, you are ready to start. Ideally, as discussed in Chapter 2, you should have your scorekeeper keep track of your pre-season games just as if they were real games. The score sheets from the pre-season games should be entered into your program to serve as the start of your data collection. Your program will let you identify the game type, so remember to label those games as pre-season games. Later in the season, you may want to delete the pre-season games' stats off the cumulative report, but early on, it is fun for the players to see their stats and begin to understand how to read the reports, etc. It is also a good chance for you and your scorekeeper to get familiar with the process. Good communication from the field to the score book to the computer is essential in stat tracking. Rest assured that your players will be checking your accuracy, and they will be quick to point out any errors when they impact their averages.

Using the program for pre-season games also gives you the opportunity to teach your players about what all the different stats mean. Use your meeting time at the end of a practice to distribute the stats, and plan some teaching time. This time is especially important in the younger age groups where it may be some of your players' first exposure to baseball statistics. TurboStats allows you to print the definitions along with brief explanations of the stats on your reports, which is highly recommended when distributing reports to your players after the early games, regardless of the age of your players (Figure 5-1).

Exactly What Do I Track?

The decision to track your team's performance requires a genuine commitment on your part. The next thing you have to decide is how extensive you want to be with your stats. A minimum number of items will be critical for you to manage your team. Beyond that minimum, the extent to which you track your statistics will be in direct proportion to the amount of time and energy you wish to invest. Most statistical programs provide more than enough stats to provide information on your team's batting, fielding, and pitching.

Offensive Stats

The primary concern when it comes to offensive stats is knowing as much as you can about your team's hitting ability. The basics will tell you what little Johnny's chances are of getting a hit each time he comes to bat. The more you collect and input, the more you will know. In addition to the basic batting average (e.g., Johnny got three hits in 10 at bats, for a batting average of .300), you will want to track the number of times Johnny gets on base by either a base on balls or a hit by pitch (some coaches incorporate sacrifice flies into this number as well), which yields a very important stat: on-base percentage. Other information will focus on how strong of a hitter he is, how many extra-base hits he gets, and how many home runs he hits. All of these numbers create an offensive picture of Johnny, which will assist you in positioning him in the lineup. The basic numbers, combined with your baseball "gut", need to be considered as you create the lineup for each game. Generally speaking, the following items should factor into putting a player higher in the batting order:
- Batting average (BA)
- On-base percentage (OBP)
- Extra-base hits (2B, 3B, HR) (*Note*: You want someone who gets a lot of extra-base hits to be the fourth batter in the lineup, otherwise known as the cleanup hitter, so

2008 ABC Records & Publishing Stats for Austin Huff #34 (ALL)
Batting Report

GAME	AB	R	H	1B	2B	3B	HR	RBI	TBB	Avg	Slg	Obp	Trend	3Avg.	Avg.rds	Cont%	OBS	G	SOL	SOS	HP	SB	Sacb	Sacf	CS	SB%	TB	HS
College Grove	2	0	2	1	1	0	0	1	2	1000	1500	1000	0	1000	0	1000	2500	1	0	0	0	0	0	0	0	0	3	1
Brentwood - Ford	3	2	3	2	0	1	0	1	1	1000	1667	1000	0	1000	0	1000	2667	1	0	0	0	1	0	0	0	1000	5	2
Brentwood - Ford	3	1	2	2	0	0	0	0	0	667	667	750	-125	875	0	667	1417	1	1	1	2	2	0	0	0	1000	2	3
Bulldogs	3	2	0	0	0	0	0	0	1	0	0	250	-364	556	0	1000	250	1	0	0	0	3	0	0	0	1000	0	0
Franklin (1)	2	1	0	0	0	0	0	0	1	0	0	500	-462	250	0	500	500	1	1	1	1	1	0	0	0	1000	0	0
Franklin (2)	1	1	0	0	0	0	0	0	1	0	0	500	-500	0	0	0	500	1	0	0	0	1	0	0	0	1000	0	0
Franklin (1)	0	2	0	0	0	0	0	1	2	0	0	1000	0	0	0	0	1000	1	0	0	1	1	0	0	0	1000	0	0
Bulldogs	1	2	1	1	0	0	0	0	2	1000	1000	1000	33	500	0	1000	2000	1	0	0	0	1	0	0	1	500	1	1
Brentwood - Ford	2	1	1	1	0	0	0	1	1	500	500	667	-4	667	0	1000	1167	1	0	0	0	1	0	0	0	1000	1	2
Brentwood 17-18	2	1	1	1	0	0	0	0	1	500	500	667	-7	600	0	500	1167	1	1	1	0	2	0	0	0	1000	1	3
Bulldogs	1	1	0	0	0	0	0	0	2	0	0	667	-33	400	0	0	667	1	1	1	0	0	0	0	0	0	0	0
Bulldogs	2	1	2	1	1	0	0	0	2	1000	1500	1000	45	600	0	1000	2500	1	0	0	0	0	0	0	0	0	3	1
Brentwood - Ford	2	1	1	0	0	1	0	0	2	500	1500	750	-4	600	0	1000	2250	1	0	0	1	2	0	0	0	1000	3	2
Total for Player	24	17	13	9	2	2	0	5	18	542	792	756	-4	600	1000	792	1547	13	4	4	3	15	0	0	1	938	19	2

[AB]-At bat in Average   [R]-Runs   [H]-Total Hits   [1B]-Single   [2B]-Double   [3B]-Triple   [HR]-HomeRun   [TBB]-Total Walks   [Avg]-Game Avg   [Slg]-Slugging%   [Obp]-On Base Average   [Trend]-Change
[3Avg.]-3Game Average   [Avgrds]-Average rds   [Cont%]-Atbats without Strike out%   [OBS]-OnBase% + Slugging%   [G]-Games   [SOL]-Strike Out Looking   [SOS]-Strike Out Swinging   [HP]-Hit
by Pitch   [SB]-Stolen Base   [Sacb]-Sac Bunt   [Sacf]-Sac Fly   [CS]-Caught Stealing   [SB%]-Stolen Base%   [TB]-Total Bases   [HS]-Hitting Streak

Figure 5-1. Report printed with the definitions included

they can help you score early in the game by bringing around the first three hitters, assuming they got on base, to score.)

- Past-three-games batting average (*Note*: This number is key since it flags players who are beginning to slump or are coming out of a slump.)
- The trend (*Note*: This number also helps to identify the beginning or end of a slump. It is represented by positive numbers for players who are trending upward in their batting average and negative numbers for those players who could be trending into a slump.)
- Player speed (*Note*: Speed should be evaluated based on timing drills and the number of stolen bases versus stolen base attempts.)

These factors, combined with your gut instinct, will yield winning lineups that can be defended if questioned by a curious parent. All of this information is intuitive and elementary, but many of your opposing coaches will not take the time to keep stats. Believe it or not, some paid coaches do not bother to study the numbers that are at their disposal. Having this kind of lackadaisical attitude will always show up in the performance of your team. Pay attention to the details, and use the previous list of six categories (five of which come from your game stats) as a minimum of offensive items to track.

It is especially important to keep in mind the speed of your runners when setting up your batting order. Some players may be excellent hitters, but slow runners. It is difficult—if not impossible—to teach speed. It *is* possible to improve a player's speed through drills and other techniques, but, generally speaking, you will not have the experience or the time to focus on improving the speed of your players. You need to focus on baseball fundamentals and skills. You and your coaches need to be aware of the slower runners and take speed into consideration as you create your batting lineup. Never place a strong hitter who is a slow runner ahead of a speed guy in the lineup because the slow runner will become a "roadblock," hampering the speedy player's attempts to steal bases or distract the opposing pitcher. The object of your #1, #2, and #3 hitters is to get on base and get around to score as quickly as possible. Your leadoff or #1 hitter should have a high on-base percentage, and he should be one of the fastest players on your roster.

Defensive Stats

If only a limited number of volunteer coaches keep offensive statistics, far fewer take the time to keep track of the defensive side of the game. Defensive stats can be developed by comparing your score book to the positions that each player played in each inning. Three things need to be tracked so you can field your best defensive lineup:

- Assists (A): when a player participates in getting an out
- Putouts (PO): when a player actually makes a play to get the batter out
- Errors (E): when a player makes a throwing, fielding, or mental error that allows a player to reach or advance on the bases that should have been a putout

By tracking these three elements, ideally in your computer program, you will be able to quickly see which players are stronger defensively. As your season progresses and as you get to know your players, your stats will become your best friend in helping you field your best defense. They will also give you the backup you need in a discussion if a parent questions you about the position his son is playing.

Speed is also an important factor on the defensive side, just as it is in determining the batting lineup. For instance, you want more speed in center field than you do in right field or left field. Your shortstop and second baseman should be quicker and faster than the players who play the corners.

Wrap-Up

Information is crucial when it comes to running a company or managing your youth baseball team. To excel at anything takes extra time and effort. Keeping good statistics, reporting personal stats to your players, and sharing team stats with your coaches is essential to separate your team from the pack.

It will not be easy, but the extra effort will pay great dividends. If your players do not know where they stand, they have nothing to judge their progress or lack thereof. You will find that the competition that is created as your players strive to improve their batting averages, and hence, their batting positions will raise the batting average of your entire team.

By being aware of your team's offensive strengths and weaknesses, you will be able to field the best offensive lineup and give your team the best chance for victory. The same idea is true for setting up your defense.

You learn about your players' *speed* by clocking their base running and their *abilities* by monitoring those key statistics in batting and fielding. With this firm information in hand, your strategy will be sound and based on facts. You will always give your team the best chance to win. If you take the easy way out and do the bare minimum of homework for your team, you can quickly become the doormat of the league.

Know Your Numbers

A ton of work is involved in keeping statistics for your team. You don't have to rely on your memory to recall these numbers at will, but as your season goes on, you will intuitively know some of the key skills of your players. You will learn who has speed, who your smart base runners are, who your good fielders are, etc. Knowledge of the basics will come into play when baseball situations present themselves.

For example, the Birds were in a tie game with our arch rival, the same team we were battling with for the lead in the league. The Birds had fought back from a two-run deficit, going into the bottom of the last inning. We were thrilled to have simply been able to tie the score and keep our hopes of a victory and the league lead alive.

We had one out when the "speedster" on our team reached first base, and then, he quickly stole second base. The next batter hit a single to left field to move speedster to third. So, we had one out, runners on the corners, and our fastest player on the team at third base. We knew our next batter was skilled at making contact with the ball. We also knew that he was a very good bunter. Knowing the speed we had at third, the squeeze bunt play came to my mind as spelled out by the situation and the ability of the Birds' players.

I traditionally coached first base and had my assistant at third handling the signals to the batters and base runners. He and I had signals that we used to communicate with each other occasionally. This situation was one of those times. We had no signal for the batter to designate a squeeze play. Instead, we used our normal bunt sign with a verbal, "Shake it up." I signaled across the infield to my assistant that I wanted to bunt, and I cupped my hands and yelled to him and the batter, "Okay now, let's shake it up!"

The stage was set, the situation was perfect, and we had practiced the execution. The runner on third took off as the pitcher made his move to home, and just as we had practiced, the batter made contact and kept the ball in play. The speedster nearly beat the pitch to home—he had scored before the other team even knew what was going on. The game was over with a final score of 4-3. The Birds won and moved into first place.

This exciting story didn't happen by accident. The bottom line is that it was made possible through the knowledge of my team's numbers. Everything was in line for perfect execution, and the ability of our team to pull out an exciting, come-from-behind victory over our rival. Get into the details of managing your team so that when situations present themselves, you improve the odds of pulling off a great play.

6

Parents—How to Keep Them on Your Side and Out of Your Hair

"The art of communication is the language of leadership."

—James Humes, presidential speech writer

When you hear volunteer coaches discussing their coaching experiences, 9 out of 10 times you will hear that the hardest part of coaching is managing the parents. They can range from the overprotective parent who's afraid little Johnny is going to get dirty or get a brush burn when he slides into home to the overzealous dad who's trying to relive his childhood through his son's athletic prowess. Sadly, on the flip side is the parent who does not care at all about what you do, and they view their child's time at the ballpark as glorified babysitting. Unfortunately, those parents are out there, but ways exist to handle them and prevent them from negatively impacting your team.

This chapter will examine the relationship between parent and coach and what steps you can take to guard against having adversarial relationships with the parents. If you keep your parent group happy, your season will be more rewarding for everyone involved. Battles with parents are lose-lose-lose propositions for the coaches, the parents, and the kids.

Parental Involvement

As discussed previously, you need to involve the parents in as many ways as possible. Encouraging their involvement in helping at practices will go a long way in making them feel a part of what you are trying to accomplish.

In the younger age groups, you will have many parents waiting at the practice to take little Johnny home, so they will be standing around watching. If you do not have anything for them to do, create something. Sometimes parents will be content just to watch, but make sure you at least offer to get them involved. They can assist in drills whether they have baseball skills or not. If you happen to be scrimmaging, they can help supervise and keep order in the dugout. Whatever the task, make them feel like they are helping.

Besides the informal request to grab a glove and help shag fly balls, formal volunteer positions are available to your parents. Some of these positions are spelled out in detail in Chapter 1, and you can add to or delete from that list to suit your individual skills and requirements. The parents who do step up not only help you in building relationships with them, but they also are a tremendous asset to the team. Managed correctly, they will make your life much better by handing the details of the more tedious tasks.

Your team mom or dad should be in charge of coordinating the following details: finding volunteers from your team to work the field's concession stand, organizing team snacks, collecting money for the team pictures, planning parties, etc. The list goes on, and by having a responsible parent in that position, not only is your life easier, but also the other parents are happier when off-the-field organization runs smoothly.

Getting assistance from your parents allows you to focus on the team—managing, motivating, teaching, and encouraging. Without that help, you will be forced to do things that will distract you from the most important aspect in your job description—the ball players.

Your assistant coaches can help during the game by seeing that the players are ready to bat and that they can find their gloves when it's time to go into the field. Practices will run smoother as your assistant coaches are positioned in various positions to run different drills. One person cannot do everything that is required. View your parents as an asset rather than a liability, and everyone will be happier in the process.

Communication

Volunteer (and even paid) coaches can sometimes be poor communicators—not as much with the players, but with the parents. Consequently, parents may find themselves in a situation where they are unsure when the next game or practice might be. Since most baseball leagues are run by volunteers, schedules are apt to change, practice times get switched around, and parents can end up in a fog.

When proper communication does not take place, parents tend to get nervous and unrest develops. The next thing you know, a parent is talking behind your back, and your support diminishes as the unrest spreads. Unfortunately, this situation is fairly common. The next few pages will help you develop a plan to effectively communicate to your parents. Parents who know what's going on are happier parents, and happier parents equal happier, healthier teams.

Your communication plan should start before your first practice. Following the draft, likely the same night, you will receive the contact information for the players you drafted. Since parents will be anxious to hear what team their sons are on, telephone every parent as soon as possible after your draft. If the player happens to answer the phone, spend a little time introducing or reacquainting yourself with him, but be sure to talk personally to his parent or guardian. Introduce yourself, tell them who your team sponsor is, and let them know you will have an important parents meeting at the end of the first practice. Let them know how important it is for at least one person from their family to attend the meeting. Inform them when and where the first practice will be and what time you would like to have them present. Make sure you provide a way for the parents to contact you if they will not be able to attend the meeting.

The outline for the parents meeting was reviewed in Chapter 1, but this meeting will be your parents' first indication of how you manage your team. Be prompt—start the meeting at the specified time, regardless of the number of parents who are present. One reason to prepare a detailed agenda (Figure 1-3) and a letter for the parents (Figure 1-4) is to be sure that you cover everything you planned to in your first meeting. You also want to have something for the parents to take home, restating what you covered in the meeting. Another good reason to prepare this material is so that any parents who were unable to attend the meeting will have access to the same information. Be diligent and make sure that you talk with at least one parent or guardian for each player. A good way to insure that you have reached everyone is to print copies and write each player's name on one of the copies, and that way, you will know if you missed anyone. The importance of this first meeting cannot be underestimated.

If you are administratively challenged, you may want to assign the responsibility of communications to someone else. However, only one person should take on this responsibility—more than one person involved can lead to miscommunication and conflicting information.

Shortly following the first practice and parents meeting, make sure that you distribute a copy of the team roster to each parent. A sample template for a roster is on the CD-ROM that is included with this book (Figure 6-1). The distribution of this information will insure that the parents know how to get in touch with each other. They may want to form car pools to practices or share rides to games. When you make copies of the roster, it is a good idea to make extra copies and keep them with you in case someone misplaces his copy.

ABC BIRDS TEAM ROSTER
2008 Brentwood Baseball Babe Ruth League

ABC
Records & Publishing

Team #3

Manager -	Rod Huff	555-4340
Coach -	Glenn Hill	555-7741
Coach -	Chuck Webb	555-3125
Team Mom-	Elizabeth Miller	555-1234

Player Name	No.	Parent	Address	City	e-Mail	Phone #	Age	Birthday
Paul Abraham	8	Bill/Lydia	68 Central Avenue	Brentwood, TN 37027	abraham@earthlink.com	555-6789	16	11/6/91
Jake Beam	6	Chuck/Julia	3008 Nolensville Road	Nolensville, TN 37135	jbeamer@unitied.com	555-3125	16	1/2/92
Keith Green	21	Cody/Kim	5333 Frontier Lane	Brentwood, TN 37027	green@spacelink.com	555-7845	16	12/20/91
Spencer Hill	00	Glenn/Vickie	6554 Inavale Lane	Brentwood, TN 37027	hillforever@comcast.com	555-7741	16	1/28/92
Austin Huff	34	Rod/Lisa	9323 Hidden Oak Dr	Brentwood, TN 37027	rodhuff@comcast.net	555-4340	16	10/21/91
Matt Haines	22	Craig/Melanie	1667 Plantation Drive	Brentwood, TN 37027	melcraig@comcast.com	555-5260	16	2/10/92
Neal Joseph	45	Hal/Martha	7345 Foxboro Drive	Brentwood, TN 37027	ukwildcatts@usabc.com	555-9870	16	4/14/92
John Knight	5	Joe/Carol	4852 Norfolk Lane	Nolensville, TN 37135	nittanylions@yahoo.com	555-4279	16	9/7/91
Norman Miller	15	John/Elizabeth	9800 Southmeade Parkway	Nashville, TN 37204	tntitans@juno.net	555-1234	15	7/18/92
Micky Norris	3	Kent/Donna	7344 Brushboro Drive	Brentwood, TN 37027	ziztopnumberone@aiii.com	555-4332	16	5/10/92
Bill Phillips	17	Peter/Nancy	9008 San Marcos Drive	Nashville, TN 37220	decorator@indesign.net	555-1991	16	5/17/92
Matt Ross	14	Eddie/Nancy	6510 Wilson Pike	Brentwood, TN 37027	cheeruk@usalink.net	555-1478	16	6/11/92
John Webb	23	Chuck/Lisa	2418 Castleman Drive	Nashville, TN 37215	webbman@usalink.net	555-3125	16	11/18/91

Age as of 7/31/08

Figure 6-1. Team roster

Another idea you may want to consider is shrinking a copy of your schedule to the size of a credit card. On the back, include an abbreviated roster with basic contact information. If you laminate these cards and give them to your parents, it provides them with easy access to that information.

This chapter discusses four different methods of communicating with your parents: telephone, handouts, email, and a website. An effective communication plan could utilize any one, or even all four, of these methods.

Telephone Communications

Usually, the quickest form of communication is the conventional telephone. However, unless you reach an actual person, the idea of leaving a voice mail is uncertain. You have no way of knowing whether or not your message was effective. Consequently, the telephone should only be used for emergency situations or changes that require a speedy delivery.

Most leagues have an automated hotline that parents can call to see if games have been postponed. If your league has such a system, make sure the parents are given that information in a variety of ways. One good way is to provide the number for them on a refrigerator magnet. Try to get your parents in the habit of calling the hotline before leaving for the ballpark—especially if there has been inclement weather in your area. If your league does not have a hotline, encourage them to install one.

In the event that no hotline is available, the best way to reach your team quickly is to develop a phone chain (Figure 6-2). The concept of a phone chain is simple. Divide your team into three or four equal groups. You, as head coach, call the first person in each group. That person calls the next person in that group, who calls the next name on the list, and so on. If someone does not answer, the person should leave a voice mail (or call back later if there is no voice mail), then continue calling names on the list until he reaches someone in person. Once he makes contact, that next person then calls the next name, and so on.

Make sure to ask the parents at one of your first meetings which phone number is best for you to reach them. With the advent of cell phones, the process of reaching people quickly has been made easier, but you need to know which number is best. If the parents both work, they may not wish to be phoned at work, but it may not be effective to leave a message for them at home if there has been a last-minute change in practice. Knowing the fastest way to reach the parents is essential for any issues that pop up. Your phone chain needs to be populated with those ideal numbers.

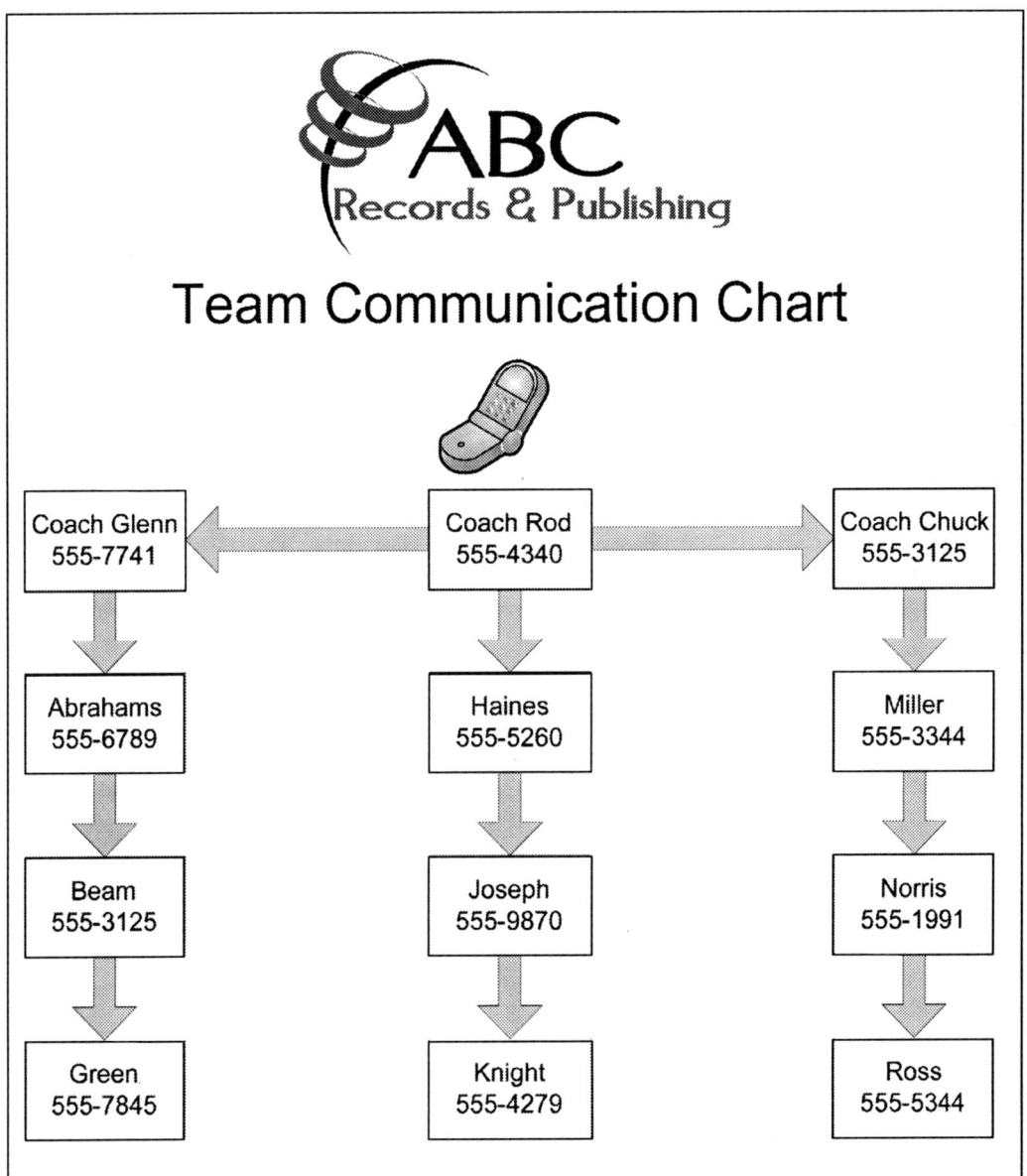

Figure 6-2. Phone chain

Another wrinkle for today's coach is the split family. You, as the coach, need to be aware of any situations where parents have split custody of one of your players. Communication can be difficult in these types of situations, so be sure to have contact information for each parent and anyone else who may be in charge of getting your player to games or practices.

Printed Handouts

Using printed handouts is an excellent vehicle to communicate with parents. A few general guidelines can make this method more effective. Since handouts usually have to pass through the hands of your players to reach the parents, one tip to help make the connection from coach to player to parent more reliable is to print your handouts on brightly-colored paper. Doing so more easily identifies the handout as something important, and if it ends up on the bottom of the player's bat bag, it will be easier for the parents to see.

Be consistent with your handouts. Use them regularly and attempt to keep a running summary of the next three or four reasons (games, practices, events, etc.) for the team to get together (Figure 6-3). Use a computer if possible, and make your handouts look as polished as possible. Including your sponsor's logo or your team's logo is a nice touch. The parents will be looking for the handouts after each gathering, and they will always know when the next practice or game is scheduled. Including several upcoming events on each handout will be helpful in the event of rain cancellations.

You need to be aware of several downsides to using handouts. Changes will play havoc once something has been put in ink, and you run the risk of people relying on information from an old handout that has been changed. It is a good practice to utilize the phone chain to emphasize anything that has been published and then changed. Good record keeping and documentation is a must. Later in this chapter, a record-keeping tip will be presented to assist the coach in organizing communications and other aspects of administration surrounding a well-run team.

Another downside to using handouts is that errors could be made when creating the handouts. If possible, have another set of eyes review what you have written. A common error is to indicate the wrong day of the week or the incorrect date. The use of word processing programs are a great aid in keeping the handouts consistent with minimal work. However, you must be careful as the ease of creation can be quickly offset if mistakes are made by not changing things appropriately. Having a good communication plan along with the use of handouts is tedious but well worth the effort. Parents tend to be unaccustomed to such detail, and they will sing your praises.

Email Communications

As more people become computer savvy, email is fast becoming a viable mode of communication. However, as with any form of communication, email has its benefits and its disadvantages.

ABC
Records & Publishing

IMPORTANT DATES

PRACTICE
Tuesday, April 15, 2008
6:00PM – Dark
Cumberland Presbyterian Church

PRACTICE
Thursday, April 17, 2008
5:30PM – 7:00PM
Granny White Park Field #2

FIRST GAME vs. COLLEGE GROVE
At Nolensville – Monday, April 21, 2008
6:00PM (Players no later than 5:30PM)

PRACTICE
Tuesday, April 22, 2008
6:00PM – Dark
Cumberland Presbyterian Church

Be sure to check the hotline (555-8310) for field conditions—when practice is at the church, we will still reference the hotline.

Figure 6-3. Typical handout

Nowadays, nearly everyone has an email address—this does not mean that everyone faithfully checks their email on a regular basis. Unless you are absolutely certain that all of your parents check and read emails, it should not be used solely.

Speed is the biggest benefit in using email communications. You can also request a receipt when someone opens your emails, but that requires careful supervision when you are handling 12 or more addresses. Early in the season, it is a good idea to use the feature that is available on most email software, requesting a return email so you know that your message has been read.

Another benefit with email is the cost. It is essentially a free way to relay your messages. The same document that you created as a handout can simply be attached to your email list and sent to everyone on your team with a few keystrokes. However, it is safer to use both forms of communicating.

When it comes to communicating with parents, you can never communicate too much. It seems that no matter how many times or how many different ways you communicate your message, someone will always say, "But, I didn't know about that practice."

Web-Based Communications

Web-based communication is perhaps the most difficult for the average coach to accomplish, but it is a very effective way to insure that the most current information is available. Many leagues are now providing this type of support for their coaches, but supplying accurate content for your team will be your responsibility.

If you are not inclined to take on this responsibility, find out if any of the parents or even one of your players is gifted with the ability to design or maintain a website. There will be a cost (unless your league provides you with free space) associated with having a web strategy. You will have to weigh the cost versus the benefit you expect to achieve.

In addition to using the web to communicate schedules and upcoming events, you can also post photographs from practices or games as well as individual and team statistics. Another plus to the establishment of a website is that it allows little Johnny's grandparents in Florida to follow his team's progress with only a few clicks of a mouse.

Administrative Organization

With all the support of your assistant coaches and parents, it is still ultimately your responsibility as head coach to insure that everything flows smoothly for your team.

Beginning with your first coaches meeting, you will be bombarded with information overload—national rules, local rules, park regulations, etc. You will accumulate player information, and before you know it, you will be drowning in paper. To help keep all of your papers together and to provide a way for you to easily find information, purchase a three-ring binder and five or eight tabs to divide your book.

Use this book to keep track of statistics, rosters, forms that track each player's innings played, etc. Quick access to this information will be beneficial as the season moves on, and it will provide you a source to answer nearly any parent question.

Include a tab for handouts, and keep copies of everything you distribute in the way of a handout or an email. Doing so will help you chronicle the season as you prepare for your year-end festivities (see Chapter 7). Since everything can be filed in this binder, it is easy for you to take to practices and games. It is readily available to answer questions and assist with memory lapses on your part. In the heat of the season, you have to be the best prepared. Your "book" will serve you well.

Wrap-Up

From your first encounter with your parents, let them know that they are a vital part of your team, and more important, a vital ingredient in their child's baseball experience. The success or failure of your team will rely on the involvement and participation not only from their children, but also from them. Find something for every parent to do who wishes to be involved.

Show the parents, time and again, that you are in control and that you have the best interest of their children in mind when you do anything. Stress that you will be doing a ton of communicating with them, but you want them to communicate with you if there is something they feel that you need to know. You want them to talk with you and not another parent if they are dissatisfied with something. Have a clear understanding on this subject from your first meeting.

Communicate with your parents in a variety of ways. Four methods of communicating were discussed in this chapter, but other ways do exist. As the head coach, it is your responsibility to coordinate all aspects of your team. You need to develop a communication strategy using any one or all of the methods described. Consistency matters, so be consistent with whatever strategy that you determine to work best in your circumstances. It is better to err on the side of too much communication than not enough.

A three-ring binder gives you with the ability to bring your records to the ball field. Be diligent with your record keeping and your mobile ballpark office.

If you are not administratively oriented, either force yourself to do so or find a reliable volunteer from your group of parents to handle this aspect of your team. The things spelled out in this chapter should not be left undone as they are extremely important in having a smooth-flowing season with satisfied parents.

Parental Support at Its Finest

Probably one of the best examples of parental support for the Birds came about one evening in the middle of a season. The Birds had an important game scheduled, and all the parents wanted to be there to cheer the boys on. Unfortunately, it was also the same day as a significant wedding anniversary for two of the parents. They were torn between celebrating their anniversary with a nice, romantic dinner or going to the ballpark to cheer for their son and the rest of the Birds.

When I arrived at the ball field, I noticed that the father was busy setting up a table down the first base line just beyond our dugout. Then, he pulled out a black linen tablecloth, and proceeded to bring out china and candles—the whole nine yards. Confused, I asked him what he was doing. He explained the situation and that he was going to surprise his wife with a romantic anniversary dinner after all—not at a fancy restaurant, but at our ballpark.

His wife arrived and was totally surprised by what her husband had done. Candles were lit, dinner was served, and the umpire called, "Play ball." Of course, all the moms were impressed by such a sweet gesture, the dads were measuring how high the bar had just been raised for them in their relationships, and the boys weren't sure what to think.

At the end of the game and after our team meeting, the Birds topped off their romantic evening at the ballpark by serenading them with a rousing chorus of *Happy Anniversary* sung to the tune of *Happy Birthday*. Yes, it was the thought that counted.

The act of kindness from a husband to his wife spoke volumes to me about their relationship, but personally, it spoke to the importance that these two parents placed on being there for their son and the rest of the Birds. They desperately wanted to be in two places at once, so they did the next best thing—they combined the two and provided a memorable experience for themselves as well as the rest of the team. To me, this act was a huge compliment and an example of parental involvement at its best.

7

Finish Strong

*"For I am already being poured out like a drink offering, and
the time has come for my departure. I have fought the good
fight, I have finished the race, I have kept the faith."*

—Paul's letter to Timothy (2 Timothy 4:6-7)

Your season is nearly complete, and depending upon your circumstances, you may be a bit weary. If you carefully followed the instructions in this book, you should feel good about how your team has come together. You should see signs of both your players enjoying themselves on the field and their parents enjoying themselves as spectators. Parents are likely hanging around after the games, replaying certain plays, reliving the funny things, and discussing the 'what ifs'. Whatever the reason, you have been successful in forming a team with faithful followers and supporters.

Coaching a team the proper way takes energy, and as the season rolls on and nears completion, you may feel a tendency to let up a little on all the details that are necessary for you to manage the team. You undoubtedly have formed a good impression in the eyes of your players and their families. Be diligent with the habits that you have developed. Do not let up at the end. You want to finish like you started—finish strong.

This chapter will help you to close out your season in a way that will leave a lasting impression on all the members of your team. Dig deep and muster the energy it is going to require. The excitement and enthusiasm that you built can be easily lost if you fizzle out at the end of the season. It will be well worth the effort that you make in the waning weeks of the season as your players will remember their experience with you as standing out from previous seasons and other coaches.

Keepsake Season Recap

An excellent way to have your players and families remember the season is to prepare a scrapbook that encapsulates the season. The book should include pages that are generic to all the books as well as individualized pages, which will both be discussed in this chapter. A template of a scrapbook is included on the companion CD-ROM. Be creative and have fun with this project. If you are not inclined to put this kind of book together, attempt to find a willing volunteer from your parent group. Someone who has the skill and the time will likely be glad to assist you or even take on the project. The memories are worth saving, and this project offers an excellent way to consolidate an entire season in 10 to 15 pages.

Keepsake Book (Generic Pages)

The generic pages will go in every player's book. Start early in the season, capturing photos of various team meetings and outings. As was suggested earlier, if you have a parent who volunteers to be your team photographer, make sure he comes to early practices with a camera. Those cold, dreary spring practices and scrimmages are all part of your team's history and should not be overlooked.

Figure 7-1. Team book cover

Pre-season parties, trips to professional baseball games, and any other team activities need to be chronicled and included on the pages of your book. Do not limit your photos to players and coaches—moms, dads, grandparents, brothers, and sisters all combine to form memories of the season.

Your pre-game rituals such as warm-ups with the players lined up down the line, pre-game talks, team prayers, and breakdown cheers are all memories of the team that are worth including. Having parents who are willing to share their photos will make this job much easier.

Encourage picture taking by all the parents. Having plenty of photos insures that none of your players gets left out. In the process of pulling your photos together, be sure to include everyone. Make the extra effort to review the selected photos. If your league does not provide a professional photographer to take pictures of your team and players, make sure that you schedule it yourself. Have fun with it. Have them take a serious traditional team picture, but then let them take a crazy picture and use both in the book.

In the era of digital photography, sharing photos and using them is simple. If you have a parent who opts to use 35mm film, you can still have those photos transferred to a disk, which will make using them less expensive. It is also possible to have the photos scanned in a format that allows you to use them on your computer. Whatever the process, capture photos of everything you can from the first practice to the last game. Those memories will be relived time and again as a result of a thoughtful photographer.

With the use of readily available software (i.e., Microsoft PowerPoint, Mircosoft Publisher, etc.), it is fairly easy to put together a professional-looking keepsake. As in other team handouts described previously, use your team logo or mascot in your presentation.

As the generic section of your books takes shape, have it edited carefully. Make sure that all names are spelled correctly and captions accurately reflect the players or parents who are in the photos. If you take on the creation of the book yourself, do not attempt to pull everything together without at least one other person to assist in the editing process. A committee of parents could help with this project, providing they are all working off the same design templates. PowerPoint and Publisher both provide very nice design templates, or you can easily create a unique template. Whatever you decide, keep one consistent template throughout your pages. Once the generic pages are together, it's time to begin to work on the more tedious part of the book.

Keepsake Book (Individual Player Pages)

The value in keeping good statistics in the management of your team has been established. At the end of the year, statistics play another vital part in the process. Having pages in individual books that are specific to that player is a great touch to an already valuable keepsake.

In addition to the statistics, you need to have someone capture a minimum of two photos of every player on your roster. One of the photos should be a typical baseball pose. The other photo or photos should capture each player in action (i.e., in the field, on the mound, or at bat). Again, this process takes diligence and planning. If you procrastinate until the last week of the season to make sure you have the right shots, inevitably, little Johnny will be on vacation that week, and he will end up without individual photos.

Place the pictures in the book in an appealing way. Fill up the individual pages with as many pictures of that player as you have since those pages will not be in everyone's book (Figure 7-2). The page immediately following the photo page should include that player's batting and fielding stats if you kept them (Figure 7-3). Your pitchers should also have their pitching stats summarized. All stats should be broken down in a game-by-game recap. Again, this task can be tedious, laborious, and time-consuming, but it is well worth the effort.

Figure 7-2. Individual photo page

ABC Records & Publishing

AUSTIN HUFF #34

GAME	AB	UP	R	H	1B	2B	3B	HR	RBI	TBB	Avg	Obp	Slg	3Avg	Trend	SO	BB	SOI	SOS	HP	Sach	Caut	Sacf	OBF	GB	HS	SB	CS	SPK
World Bridge	3	3	2	2	1	1	0	0	3	0	667	667	1000	667	0	0	0	0	0	0	0	0	0	0	0	1	0	0	0
World Bridge	2	4	2	1	0	0	0	0	1	2	500	750	500	500	-67	1	2	1	0	0	0	0	1	0	2	3	0	1000
Bulldogs	2	2	0	1	1	0	0	0	2	0	500	500	500	571	-95	1	0	1	0	0	0	0	0	3	0	0	0	
Casa Fiesta	3	3	3	1	2	0	0	0	1	0	1000	1000	1667	714	129	0	0	0	0	0	0	0	1	4	2	0	1000	
Premier Orthopedic	2	3	1	0	0	0	0	0	1	0	333	0	571	-117	2	1	0	2	0	0	0	0	0	2	0	1000		
O'Charley's	2	3	2	1	1	0	0	0	0	0	500	667	500	571	-125	1	0	0	1	0	0	0	0	1	0	1000		
Pan Am Electric	2	3	3	2	1	0	1	0	2	1	1000	1000	2000	500	54	0	1	0	0	0	0	0	2	1	0	1000		
Bulldogs	2	3	1	0	0	0	0	0	1	0	333	0	500	-69	2	1	1	1	0	0	0	0	0	0	0			
Bulldogs	2	3	1	0	0	0	0	0	1	1	0	333	0	333	-125	1	1	0	1	0	0	0	0	0	0	0		
World Bridge	1	3	3	1	1	0	0	0	0	2	1000	1000	1000	200	24	0	2	0	0	0	0	0	1	2	0	1000		
Pan Am Electric	2	3	2	1	0	0	1	0	0	0	333	333	333	571	-7	0	0	0	0	0	0	0	2	0	0			
O'Charley's	3	3	0	0	0	0	0	0	0	0	0	0	333	-62	3	0	2	1	0	0	0	0	1	0	0			
Premier Orthopedic	3	3	1	1	1	0	0	0	0	0	333	250	-76	2	0	2	0	0	0	0	0	0	1	0	0			
Casa Fiesta	3	4	0	0	0	0	0	0	0	1	0	250	0	111	-119	1	1	1	0	0	0	0	0	1	0	0		
Pan Am Electric	2	4	3	1	0	1	0	0	3	1	500	500	1000	250	6	0	1	0	0	0	1	1	1	1	0	0		
O'Charley's	1	4	1	0	0	0	0	0	0	3	0	750	0	167	-12	0	3	0	0	0	0	0	0	1	0	1000		
World Bridge	2	3	1	1	2	1	0	0	0	1	1000	1000	1500	600	32	0	1	0	0	0	0	0	0	0	0		
World Bridge	2	3	2	1	1	0	0	0	0	1	500	667	500	600	36	1	1	1	0	0	0	0	0	2	2	0	1000
Bulldogs	3	3	1	1	1	0	0	0	0	0	333	333	333	571	-7	2	0	0	2	0	0	0	0	3	1	0	1000
Casa Fiesta	1	3	1	0	0	0	0	0	0	2	0	667	0	333	-17	0	2	0	0	0	0	0	0	1	0	1000	
World Bridge	2	2	0	0	0	0	0	0	0	0	0	0	167	-36	1	0	1	0	0	0	0	0	0	0	0		
Total for Player	45	65	29	18	11	5	2	0	13	18	400	569	600	167	-36	19	18	8	11	1	0	2	1	2	2	0	16	0	1000

Figure 7-3. Individual stats page

Complete Team Book

You do not want to prepare a book for every player that includes the individual statistics of the other players. Some players may not want their stats shared with everyone, so be sensitive to that fact. However, understanding the expense and time involved, it is valuable to prepare a complete team book (i.e., one that includes every individual player page) for each of your assistant coaches to keep as a memory of the season. You may also want to select a few "friends of the program" that you wish to honor by presenting them with a complete book. A grandparent who was a faithful fan and friend of the players will be touched by the fact that you recognized him with a book of the entire team.

End-of-the-Year Party

Volunteer coaches tend to put little effort into a year-end party, but your players deserve to have a celebration. A trip to a local fast-food establishment would be better than doing nothing, but try to do something more if possible. If you followed the guidelines in the earlier chapters, you have equipped yourself with a willing team mom or dad. Call upon this person and other volunteers to help you put together a memorable event.

Have some type of program prepared so it's not just a social affair. If you prepared your scrapbooks using PowerPoint, you can project the pictures on the wall or a screen using a projector. Project the pages for each individual player as you call them to the front of the room for their time in the spotlight.

If you had a successful season, your team may have already been presented trophies by the league. If not, or in addition to, you may want to collect money from the parents to buy a small trophy to present to each player at the party.

Another alternative is to create certificates on your computer and personalize them for each player (Figure 7-4). If you go this route, make sure you have an award for each player. Awards such as "most improved player" or "most energetic player" can be used if you have difficulty coming up with appropriate awards for everyone. The important thing is that you *must* find something to say about each player as they are called to the front. You don't want to lie, and you may have to dig deep, but you can always find something worth mentioning for every player. You may want to use the same kind of certificate to recognize special fans like a granddad who didn't miss any games, etc. Keep this party in mind throughout the season, and keep notes about things you want to remember at the end of the season.

Figure 7-4. Sample certificate

If you do create a team book to present to special people who supported your team throughout the season, make sure they get a special invitation to the party. It is more meaningful to the recipients if the appreciation of the players and parents can be demonstrated in person.

This party is also a good place for you to recognize your assistant coaches and the volunteer parents who stepped up to take on those important jobs. A framed team picture with a personalized note on the back or some other memento is a good choice for those people. Your sponsor may contribute a gift or cash to defray the cost of the party.

Be sensitive of the time and keep your comments minimal. Remember that you have 10 to 12 players to highlight, and the presentations to assistants, parent volunteers, and other supporters can make for a long program if you are not careful. You want them to remember the season, not how long-winded your presentations were.

Create a fun atmosphere for the program, maybe even with decorations. Be organized and take time beforehand to make sure everyone who is participating knows his role. Time how long it takes, and cut down where you need to. Keep the program tight, and do not go longer than 45 minutes with your formal presentation. Keep your event lighthearted and have fun.

Wrap-Up

At this point in the season, the time likely seemed to fly by. You may be getting tired— being a *great* volunteer coach takes a lot of energy. Be encouraged that you *are* making a lasting impression on the young players who look to you as a role model. Do not underestimate that position of authority.

Dig deep to find the energy to finish your program strong. This point in the season can really separate you from the pack. Taking the time and effort it takes to create a scrapbook for each player is rare among volunteer coaches. The books become permanent keepsakes for your players and parents. They will be shared with cousins, aunts, uncles, grandparents, and even the players' own children down the road. Remember, as you take the necessary time to create these books that they will always maintain a special place on your players' bookshelves.

Likewise, the end-of-the-year party can put the finishing touch on a successful season, regardless of your win-loss record. Try to find a place to make it special. A parent may volunteer their backyard pool, or you may find a restaurant that has a private room. The place is not as important as the time and energy that goes into planning it. Carefully plan your event, and make sure that the important people you wish to recognize can be present for the event.

You need to prepare your comments before you arrive at the event, and make sure every player has a moment in the spotlight. That preparation will help you avoid an awkward moment when you forget little Johnny's name or what position he played. Those slip-ups do happen, and they are difficult to overcome.

The bottom line of this chapter is to finish your season strong—do not fail to exert a little extra effort when the end is in sight. You will never regret the time that you put into making your season memorable.

An Exceptional End-of-the-Year Party

Year-end parties for the Birds were always something that the players, the parents, and the extended families looked forward to. Over the years, they ran the gamut from pizza at a local restaurant to pool parties to banquet halls.

For several years toward the end of my active coaching days, we were blessed with a player on our team who was talented, pleasant, and a real asset to our team. In addition to the blessing of their son, his parents owned a catering business and a fully-equipped banquet hall that was used for wedding receptions, corporate gatherings, etc. When the time came at the end of one of our most successful seasons, they approached me about having the end-of-season party at their hall.

The more I thought about the idea, the more interested I became in doing something totally out of the ordinary for a year-end team party. I agreed to have the party at their facility, and they took it from there. The boys and parents showed up and were greeted by tuxedo-garbed servers, candlelight, table linens, and china. The food was amazing, and everyone was blown away by what this set of parents had done for the Birds. They even had a screen set up for my awards presentation—everything was perfect.

It could have been the setting, or maybe the ragtag group of players who came together as a team to post an undefeated season, or the great turnout we had, including the league president, the players, the families, and several grandparents, but that night was the most emotional of my coaching career. Like I said, it could have been any one of those factors, but I'm convinced that the most moving ingredient of the night was the fact that these two parents cared enough about me and our team to go above and beyond the call of duty to create a night that no one would forget.

The clincher of the night was that they refused to accept any money from anyone to help them with the cost of the event. That gesture spoke volumes to me and our team. Their response to my expression of gratitude was that we had made such a lasting impression on their son, and that no amount of money, food, or whatever could ever repay me and my assistant coaches for the job we had done that season. They would never forget that team, the friends they made on the sideline, and the joy in their son's eyes when he was a part of the Birds.

8

The Last Inning

"The leaders who work most effectively, it seems to me, never say 'I'. And that's not because they have trained themselves not to say 'I'. They don't think 'I'. They think 'we'; they think 'team'. They understand their job to be to make the team function. They accept responsibility and don't sidestep it, but 'we' gets the credit.... This is what creates trust, what enables you to get the task done."

—Peter Drucker

"My heritage to my children isn't words or possessions, but an unspoken treasure of my example as a man and a father. More than anything I have, I'm trying to pass that on to my children."

—Will Rogers

A lot of information has been presented on the preceding pages. The tendency may be to become overwhelmed and not implement anything. The challenge is to push through that feeling and commit to making yourself a better coach, and as a result, provide a more enjoyable experience for your players and their families.

This chapter is an attempt to pull the information from this book together and summarize the key points from each chapter. When you volunteer to become a coach, chances are that your commitment will end up being for more than one season. Your agreement to help out "this season" usually turns into a commitment that spans your child's entire time in the league. With that understanding, you may not want to attempt to tackle everything in this book during your first season as a coach. However, the more you take on and accomplish, the more experience you will gain and the better experience your players and families will have.

Pre-Season Preparation

The kind of talent that you have to work with for the season will be determined at that initial meeting where your league pulls all the coaches together to conduct the traditional draft. Every league has variations to their rules for conducting this pre-season ritual, so become familiar with the rules prior to the draft meeting. Call the person who recruited you to coach, or check with the league president or commissioner, but whatever you do, know how the process will take place so you are not at a disadvantage. If your assistant coach is allowed to participate, make sure he can attend. The more knowledge you have at your disposal the better.

Study the tryout sheets, but pay attention to the age of the players as well. An older player who had slightly lower scores at the tryout than a younger player may turn out to be a better overall player as a result of his age. Players with older siblings who play the game tend to be more talented than their brothers were at their age.

Remember that some players do not do well in tryout situations, so some players who are rated lower in the draft may prove to be very valuable during the season. If you recognize a player with that kind of potential, draft him early—if you are familiar with him, chances are that another coach in the room has spotted him as well.

Sometimes, it is wise to draft more for the parents than the player. What this statement means is that if you know the parents are supportive and friendly, chances are they will have that same attitude toward you and your team. Great volunteers are not always easy to find, and a good team is made up of more than just the players.

Immediately following the draft, call each player personally and attempt to talk with both a parent and the player, and arrange for that all-important first practice and meeting. The first practice and parents meeting need to be scheduled on the same night. You have only one chance to make that valuable first impression, so you need to mind the details of that first event.

Your first practice should be low key, with a strong emphasis on getting to know your players and assessing how their skills align with what was on the tryout sheet. You will likely be surprised by the results—great players who did not tryout well and weaker players who got lucky. Attempt to do some things that help the players get to know each other. The quicker they get to know each other, the quicker they can begin to gel as a team. Playing a game that awards baseball cards to anyone who can name each of the other players successfully is a good icebreaker and can accomplish this goal nicely.

Plan to have the parents meeting during the last half hour of your practice time, and have a plan in place to meet, one-on-one if necessary, with any families who did not have a representative at the meeting. It is important that everyone hears the same message and information from you. Rely on handouts as a memory jogger and a way to keep consistent. Make your handouts professional looking by using a computer—templates are available on the CD-ROM that is included with this book. If your team has a sponsor or a mascot, attempt to utilize the sponsor's logo or an image of your mascot in all handouts that you prepare.

Use this meeting time to carefully explain the job descriptions of the parent volunteers that you need to support the team throughout the season. No better time exists to firm up these positions than at the first meeting. Do not force volunteers, as that is sometimes worse than not having volunteers at all. Presented properly, with a clear definition of your expectations, you will likely find a willing candidate for each of your jobs.

Building a Team

Beginning with your first practice, make every effort to insure that your team members know each other by name. This point is especially important if you draw players from various schools. Guard against schoolmates forming cliques on your team. This habit can be disastrous as no common bond will be formed, and you will have several mini-teams instead of one strong team.

Another *must* is to schedule some kind of off-the-field event prior to your first game. Having a sleepover with pizza and a movie can go a long way in creating a sense of team. Watching an inspirational sports movie (preferably a baseball film, though not mandatory) is a good way to get them thinking *team*.

Always have team meetings outside the dugout before the start of each game and after every defensive inning. Do a breakdown cheer such as, *"Team* on three...one, two, three...*team,"* substituting your mascot or some other word for the word *team*. A time of prayer or quiet meditation is always good to schedule into your pre-game meetings. Have these meetings at a consistent time, preferably just prior to taking the field if you are the home team, or before you go to bat if you are the visiting team. The first meeting of the game should follow all of your pre-game rituals of stretching and warming up.

Encourage the parents to attend the games and support the players. Provide lineup cards for the parents with the names and numbers of all the players so they can familiarize themselves with the team and get more involved. Use the spreadsheet that is included in the roster template on the companion CD-ROM to create your own "Parents' Guide" (Figure 8-1).

Parent's Guide

Name	#
Micky Norris	3
John Knight	5
Jake Beam	6
Paul Abraham	8
Matt Ross	14
Norman Miller	15
Bill Phillips	17
Keith Green	21
Matt Haines	22
John Webb	23
Austin Huff	34

Figure 8-1. Parents' guide

Make It Fun for Everyone

Truthfully, winning *does* matter, but it is definitely more important that your players have fun during the season. The victory of having your team look forward to practices and games is just as rewarding as a victory on the field. A team that enjoys practicing will perform better than a team that finds it a drudgery.

Add humor to your discussions with the players and the parents. A relaxed, but purposeful, environment makes for productive times when you are together as a team. Humor, not foolishness, is helpful in giving your players an opportunity to have fun. Giving out player nicknames can also add an element of fun, providing, of course, that the nicknames chosen are not derogatory in any way to the recipient.

To keep things interesting and fun at practices, it is a good idea to invite other people in to assist occasionally or provide some motivational thoughts. Your guests can range from high school stars to retired players who may reside in your area. High school coaches from other sports or youth pastors can do a great job touching on interesting points that can inspire your team.

Numbers Make the Difference

Finding a competent, reliable, and accurate scorekeeper is essential as you compile the stats from your score book using TurboStats software (or any other method) to create reports to distribute to your assistant coaches and your players. Boys of all ages *and* their dads can be very competitive. Tracking individual stats is a way to develop a competitive spirit for the betterment of your team. If little Johnny is batting last in the order, he may encourage his mom or dad to take him to the batting cages to improve his skills—and as individuals improve, so does the team.

Know your players through their stats. Recognize which players are the speedsters and the good hitters and fielders, and manage your team just as you would manage your personal life or your job. What distinguishes a great coach from a mediocre one is directly related to how much time he invests in the trade.

Be prepared for the game before you arrive at the field. Once you get to the ballpark, you will be distracted in a number of ways, so have your lineup and at least the first inning defensive lineup in place. If you wait until you arrive at the field to prepare, you will not take the necessary time to do it right.

Motivation, Motivation, Motivation

Just as location, location, location are the three most important ingredients of a real-estate deal, motivation is essential for a successful team. This idea holds true at every level of coaching, but when you are dealing with sensitive, young, insecure players in the age groups we are talking about in this book, it is crucial. You motivate and make sure that your assistant coaches and volunteer helpers are all on the same page when it comes to maintaining a positive atmosphere at practices, games, and even off-the-field events and gatherings.

End-of-the-Year Party

Try to do more than a trip to the local McDonald's to honor your players and volunteers at the end of the season. With the help of your coaches and perhaps a few trusted parents, get together to identify a way to recognize every player on your team. With the use of Microsoft products (i.e., PowerPoint or Publisher), it is easy to make customized certificates that you and your assistant coaches can sign. These individual awards should be given in addition to any trophy that your league may provide.

As you present the individual awards, take some time to talk about each player. Time and preparation are involved in putting this event together, but you are making lasting memories. This party is also a great time to present each player with the team scrapbook that you put together.

A small gift presentation to your assistant coaches and volunteers is a nice touch—one that could make finding volunteers the next year easier. A simple gift idea is to frame a team picture with a detailed game-by-game scoring summary on the back. It's not so much the gift, but the thought that counts.

Final Wrap-Up

At this point, you should be ready to take on the challenge of molding a group of kids who may or may not know each other into a team. A cohesive group of young men who, with the support their parents and other relatives, will put together a season to remember. As you carefully manage your team, you will be able to give them the best chance of putting a winning team on the field, and certainly, the best chance of having an enjoyable season.

The efforts that you decide to make on behalf of your players will be rewarding for you as well. It's not easy, and it takes countless hours of preparation, thought, and prayer. You are shaping the lives of young people, and it's possible, in those few brief months, that you could have a life-changing impact on one of your players. If nothing else, you have participated in the creation of lifelong memories. Nearly everyone can recall a coach or two from his past who made a tremendous impression and imprint on his life. By taking the extra effort and doing a few of the things mentioned in this book, the chances are better for you to make one of those kinds of impressions.

In coaching youth baseball, just as in life, you get out of it what you put into it. Take the challenge, and be prepared to make some memories. Play ball!

Be Fair to Your Own Child

A book geared toward helping volunteer coaches become better coaches would not be complete without some words of wisdom directed at dads who are attempting to coach their sons on the ball field. Most of us who have been summoned to help the local team have responded to the call due to a small set of pleading eyes, looking to us for help. Nine out of ten times, those eyes belong to a son or daughter whom you love dearly.

Coaching your own child brings about another set of challenges. I encourage you to avoid two particular pitfalls at all costs: showing favoritism to your child at the expense of other players on the team, and being harder on your child to avoid showing favoritism. An example of each of these two extremes will be presented for your consideration.

My son was in his third year of playing soccer when he was placed on a team that was coached by the star player's father. The saddest part of this story was that the coach's son was truly a gifted player. That being said, the coach *never* benched his son—he played every single period the entire season. Even after incidents that earned his son a warning card from the referees, his son stayed on the field. This favoritism became a source of irritation for the other parents, and it was discouraging to the other young players. The worst part of the story was that the coach presented his son with a special award at the end-of-the-year party, amidst gasps from the other parents in attendance. The award came at the end of a flowery speech from the coach about his son's value to the team. My son hung up his soccer shoes for the last time following this experience.

Please avoid the trap of using your position as coach to elevate your child to a position that he has not earned. An old adage exists in youth baseball: *If the coach has a son, the team has a pitcher.* Guard yourself against this temptation, and be aware of the opposite end of this spectrum. I have to confess that I have fallen into the trap being tougher on my child than he deserves.

Having witnessed the sentiment of the parents toward our soccer coach's future "David Beckham," I was overly sensitive about showing special treatment to my son. My son was one of the more-talented players on my team. The process of awarding game balls can sometimes be a challenge. Since my son is a good athlete, I would tend to overlook a great play or hit of his and choose a lesser accomplishment of little Johnny's, knowing that I may have a difficult time coming up with another reason to award him the coveted game ball.

This habit got me in trouble with my son's mother (i.e., my wife), during a season that I purposely overlooked our son's great accomplishments and opted for recognizing several of little Johnny's hits and hustles. I always had a practice of not awarding a second game ball to anyone until everyone received their first. I had awarded 11 game balls, and it was my son's time to get his. You are probably ahead of me here, but the twelfth game was one of the worst games my son had played in all my years of coaching him. What I feared happening to little Johnny had happened to my son. I was forced to make up a lame reason to award him with his postgame prize.

I'm not sure how many parents really comprehended what had happened, but he and my wife certainly did. He made a habit of writing down the date and getting the coaches to sign his game ball every time he was awarded one. He also noted on the ball the reason for the recognition. This particular ball sits in his room atop a bowl full of game balls, and it serves as a reminder of the error of my ways. On this ball, my son wrote, *I got the game ball because I was the only player who had not gotten one.* Ouch!

Be careful, and try to treat your child the same as you treat other players on your team. Your son may be the best pitcher on your team—don't be afraid to utilize his skills for the sake of the team. Likewise, don't force your son into a position that he doesn't rightfully belong. Remember, above all else, your relationship with your wife and child is more important than any game, team, or season.

A

Appendix: League Management and Responsibilities

"Good management is the art of making problems so interesting and their solutions so constructive that everyone wants to get to work and deal with them."

—Paul Hawken, environmentalist, entrepreneur, journalist, author

It is typical in business to reward the strong, efficient performers with more responsibilities. The same concept is true in youth baseball. As you adopt the procedures and systems presented in this book, people will notice that you are a different type of coach. The league will receive requests from little Johnny's parents to have him placed on your team, and other words of praise will come your way. The good news is that the league will take note of this recognition. The bad news is that you will be asked to take on various leadership roles in your league.

Although you may find you can easily handle the added responsibility, be careful not to let it distract you from focusing on your team. Generally, leagues are set up with a commissioner (the title will vary from league to league) who oversees the entire league—all age groups. The commissioner usually does not coach a team since this position carries a multitude of duties and responsibilities. Under the league commissioner are usually league presidents (titles may vary) for each of the various age groups. These positions are usually the kind of added responsibility that is taken on by a coach of one of the teams in that age group.

In the event that you decide to take on such a responsibility, the tips in this chapter should help make this job more manageable. The league presidents of each age group are generally responsible for the following activities during the season, which will be discussed in this appendix.

- Compiling a list of coaches from the people who volunteered at the league sign-ups
- Participating in and recruiting other coaches to assist in the player tryouts
- Scheduling and preparing handouts for the team drafts in conjunction with the commissioner
- Creating and distributing the practice and game schedules
- Dealing with any disputes or protests that arise during the season
- Organizing, scheduling, and administering postseason tournaments for your age group

Coach Selection

Following the player sign-ups, the volunteers will compile a list of the players who signed up to participate in the league. They will also develop a list of any parents who volunteered to coach. This task will be your first and most important task as president for your age group. Similar to the importance of drafting the right players for your team, aligning the best coaches to the right teams is critical to the success of your league.

Just as in coaching your team, communication is crucial with the coaches you select. Review the list of volunteers carefully. Time spent on this process will pay huge dividends as your season progresses. Make a point to have phone interviews or face-to-face discussions with these potential volunteers—some of whom you may never have met. A coach can make or break a season for the players, and care needs to be taken in the selection. The ideal situation is when your league has more volunteers than it has spots to fill. If you do not find yourself in this situation, you may want to consider looking for more volunteers, just so you are not forced to settle on the first people who signed up.

In the process of contacting the prospective coaches, pay attention to how easy it is for you to get in touch with each person. If you have difficulty making contact with someone, it is likely communication may continue to be a challenge as the season progresses. Give the volunteer some slack as you may have caught him on a busy day, but leaving repeated messages without receiving a return call is a bad sign.

When you do connect with a prospective coach, present hypothetical situations and ask how they would handle them. Their answers will give you insight on how they will manage their team. Ask about other coaching or teaching experience they have that would be applicable to your league. Do not hesitate to ask for references, and check out a few if you have any questions in your mind following your meetings.

Remember, you are selecting your coaches based on two things: how well you can work with this person, and how well this person deals with the parents and the players.

Both are very important, but weigh the parent/player interaction heavier than your league responsibilities. As soon as your coaches are lined up, it's time to organize your first coaches meeting and player tryouts.

Organizing Tryouts

The accuracy of the player tryouts is the most important aspect of a successful draft. During the tryouts, you will attempt to place a numeric evaluation on the basic aspects of baseball: fielding ground balls, fielding fly balls, hitting, throwing, and pitching (optional). Generally, players are rated on a scale of 1 to 10 on each of these aspects of the game.

To provide reliable evaluation numbers to your coaches, you should attempt to do the following two things: have the same coaches do the evaluations for the entire tryout, and have more than one coach at each tryout station so you can average the players' numbers.

It is important to conduct a pre-tryout meeting and stress consistency in each of the areas. For instance, for your coaches who are evaluating hitting, make sure you throw the same number of pitches to each batter and keep track of contact and power. Batters with a 1 or a 10 rating will be somewhat easy to determine. The tricky part comes in the ratings from 2 to 9. If you have the same coach evaluating the hitting station all day and you have multiple coaches rating the players, it should net you an accurate evaluation, ranking your players from top to bottom in regard to hitting abilities.

With fielding and throwing evaluations, be consistent with the number of ground balls, pop-ups, and fly balls that you hit to each player. Evaluate outfield and infield separately, and average the total scores for fielding and throwing into one number. Have the grounders fielded and thrown to first base, and have the fly balls fielded and thrown to a target or a player near the person hitting the fly balls. Have different coaches evaluating the fielding and throwing if you have enough volunteers. If not, one coach could handle both evaluations if required.

Inevitably, due to various circumstances, some players will not be able to make it to the tryout day. The first option, in this case, should be for you and several other coaches to conduct a makeup tryout for these players. If you still have missing players, as the league president, you need to get on the phone and try to ascertain the skill levels of these players. If they are new to the area, try to determine what positions they played before, and you may have to use an educated guess to assign a number to these players. If they played in your league the previous year, check the results from that year's tryouts. Whatever you do, you must have an evaluation number for every player in the draft.

Computers are a necessity when compiling this data, as you will be working with many numbers. You should end up with one numerical evaluation for each player in each of the three main categories: hitting, fielding, and throwing. Combine these three scores, yielding a total score of 0 to 30 for each player. Then, sort the names by total score in descending order to determine each player's ranking number (which will be used instead of the player's name during the draft), and give a copy to each of your coaches at the draft. (*Note:* If more than one player has the same total score, rank them alphabetically by last name.)

In addition to the numerical evaluations, other information should be included in the evaluation sheet that will be used in the draft. A code must appear that indicates the following:

- CS (coach's son): Protects a coach's son from being erroneously drafted by another team.
- BR (brothers): Indicates that the player has a brother in the draft, so the drafting of that player automatically includes the brother. Leagues establish this rule as a courtesy to parents who have more than one child playing.
- SP (sponsor): Indicates that the player's father/mother has expressed an interest in sponsoring a team.
- NE (no evaluation): Indicates that the player did not go through the normal evaluation process, and his evaluation was determined by other means.

Managing the Draft

Assemble your coaches in a room that provides a place for them to have a writing surface. Many leagues have a meeting room, but if yours doesn't, try to find a local business that will let you use their conference room or look for a neighborhood clubhouse you can use. Talk personally to every coach to make sure they can attend the meeting—nothing is worse than to try to conduct a draft with a missing coach.

Distribute an evaluation list to each team, and plan on 20 to 30 minutes for the coaches to review the lists before you kick off the draft. Following the review time, carefully discuss the instructions for the draft. A sample memo summarizing these instructions is available on the CD-ROM that comes with this book. A sample evaluation worksheet is also included for your convenience. Due to the sensitive nature of the information included on these evaluation lists, they should be returned to you at the conclusion of the draft.

You have already determined, based on the league sign-ups, how many teams you will field, and you have at least one head coach for each team. Prepare slips of paper with a corresponding number for each of the teams in your league and place them in a hat. Pass the hat around and have each coach pull out a number. That number represents the order in which that team will select a player in the first round. The number also becomes that team's number for scheduling purposes. In round two, the order is reversed, and the team that selected last picks first in the second round.

Remember to go over the coding mentioned previously. Coach's sons (CS) can only be drafted by the father, brothers (BR) are drafted in pairs, and if the coach does not have his own sponsor, he should try to draft a sponsor's child (SP) in the course of the draft. Make sure that two SPs do not land on the same team. Mention how the NEs (no evaluations) were actually evaluated so that the coaches realize the subjectivity involved in that number.

To monitor the progression of the draft, use a draft tally sheet (Figure A-1). When drafting a player, have the coaches use the player's ranking number (i.e., the ranking he was assigned based on his total evaluation score) rather than his name. Insert the numbers adjacent to the team number as the coaches select their players. This process serves as a great historical record of how the draft transpired, and it is a good way to backtrack in the event of an error. A template of a draft tally sheet is included on the companion CD-ROM.

To make your administrative task a bit easier, use a form to collect the player information from each team (Figure A-2). Be sure they submit a completed form to you prior to leaving the draft. A template of the form is included on the companion CD-ROM.

To allow the teams to start practicing immediately, have your practice field times available to sign up for that evening. Have the team that picked last in the first round select their practice time first, and work your way back up the team numbers until everyone has selected their times.

Brentwood Babe Ruth 11- & 12-Year-Old Draft Tally Sheet
Friday, March 14, 2008

Coach	Team #	Draft #	1	2	3	4	5	6	7	8	9	10	11	12
	1	1												
	2	2												
	3	3												
	4	4												
	5	5												
	6	6												
	7	7												
	8	8												
	9	9												

Write the player's evaluation number in the space indicated following each team's draft choice.

Figure A-1. Draft tally sheet

Team Sponsor	
Team #	

Head Coach	
Phone #	

Asst. Coach	
Phone #	

Round	Player Name	#	Phone
1			
2			
3			
4			
5			
6			
7			
8			
9			
10			
11			
12			

Figure A-2. Draft worksheet

Scheduling

Your league will provide you a listing of the fields that are available for your age group. This information allows you to take the first step in preparing your schedule. Many leagues have invested in scheduling software that makes the scheduling task much easier. In most cases, you simply enter in the available time slots, the fields that have been allocated to you, and some other parameters, and the program creates your schedule.

Without this tool, scheduling can be challenging as you try to balance the scheduling of early morning games evenly, the number of games in any week evenly, etc. You may want to enlist the assistance of another coach or two if this process has to be done manually, so if anyone complains about their game schedules, you can assure them it was done as fairly as possible.

After your game schedules have been made, you need to inform the people in charge of scheduling umpires of your schedule. The umpire scheduling could potentially fall on your shoulders, depending upon the organization of your league.

Tournament Management

The last major responsibility you will have as head of your age group is to organize the postseason tournament. You should call a meeting of your coaches just prior to the formulation of the tournament. Decisions to be made at that meeting include whether it will be single or double elimination, what kind of substitution rules you will follow (vacations start to impact many teams toward the end of the season, and some leagues stipulate a maximum number of substitutes), the pitching rules to establish (these could change for tournament play), and any other tournament issues. Pitching limitations are often mandated by your league's governing body (i.e., Little League, Babe Ruth, etc.). You need to make sure that all the coaches fully understand the difference between the tournament rules and the regular-season rules.

Teams should be seeded based on their results in the league during the regular season, and then, you can create the brackets. Again, programs are available to assist in creating tournament brackets, and many governing bodies offer these sample brackets on their websites. As in scheduling, the first thing to do is secure the field dates and times that your age group has been allocated.

Create a bracket that can be copied and distributed to the coaches. A nice touch is to take the bracket to a local copy store and have it blown up and mounted for easy display at the field during the tournament. This area becomes a place to congregate and replay the games, and it also serves as a place for you to post any key announcements. Rainouts can cause havoc when you have a limited amount of time to get all of your games in, so a central bulletin board becomes the source of quick information.

Plan an awards celebration following the championship game so the teams can be recognized for their achievements. As league president, you need to take an active role in the festivities, but as a coach, you hope your team will be there to receive trophies as well. For this reason, it's always good to have the head of the entire league scheduled to host the proceedings.

Proper Communication

As in the management of your own team, communication is key between you and the other head coaches. To avoid misinterpretation, always put your communication in writing. Be as clear and concise as possible as your coaches are busy people. You will learn which ones of your coaches are good at email communications. Do *not* rely on email unless you are *certain* your coaches will read correspondence via email. Probably, the best way to insure that your coaches receive information is to print out the memo, write each coach's name on a copy, and hand it to each one personally. As the league president, the best way to do accomplish this task is to show up when the teams are scheduled for practice or a game.

Wrap-Up

You did an extraordinary job coaching and managing your team, and favorable comments caused the league leadership to notice that you were a special coach who really had his act together. You incorporated many of the tips and ideas you picked up in this book, and as a reward, you have been asked by your league to take on the responsibility of managing an age group. The items identified in this Appendix will assist you in that task. Don't be afraid of the responsibility, but make sure that your team is your first priority throughout the season. Your players and parents should not suffer as a result of you accepting greater responsibilities. If you decide to take the position, you should focus on doing the best job possible.

About the Author

Rod Huff is a successful business executive with 30 years experience in the operations and administration area. He began his baseball coaching experience as an assistant coach when his son, Austin, was five years old. His first head coaching experience began in 1995 when his company, Sparrow Records, sponsored his 7- and 8-year-old coach-pitch team. That year, as a first-year coach, his team, nicknamed the Birds, went 15-2. That season ushered in somewhat of a dynasty in his Brentwood, Tennessee, community, where he is known as one of the winningest coaches ever in the local league. His nine-year record as a head coach includes five league championships and four runner-up titles.

Huff took his operational and administrative executive abilities to the ball field and came up with a winning formula of organization, feedback, and motivation, which had parents and players alike asking to be drafted by him every year. The details of his teams' success can be seen in the following chart. His teams won a minimum of one trophy from the league every year, with the exception of 1997. His players have labeled this year the "purple year," as this was the first and only year that the color of their team jerseys varied from their traditional teal.

Huff ended his coaching career following an unprecedented undefeated regular season in 2003. Their only two losses came during the postseason in a double-elimination tournament that found the Birds wounded and missing their starting shortstop, catcher, second baseman, and two pitchers—a tough way to end a season.

Academically, the author holds a Bachelor of Arts degree in economics from Shippensburg University in Pennsylvania and a Master of Business Administration from James Madison University in Harrisonburg, Virginia. He resides in Brentwood, Tennessee, with his wife of 36 years, Lisa, who is a well-known interior designer in the Nashville area. They have two children, a son, Austin, who is a senior at the University of Missouri, majoring in broadcast journalism, and a daughter, Whitney, who is a recent graduate of the University of Kentucky in Lexington, Kentucky. Huff has had the joy of seeing both of his children run onto Division I football fields—his daughter as a cheerleader at UK, and his son as a Mizzou football player. He values his family life, and is a deacon in his local church in Tennessee.

Birds' Lifetime Record

Year	League	W	L	T	%	Trophies
1995	7-8 Year Old	15	2		88.2%	League Champion
1996	9-10 Year Old	15	4	2	76.2%	Tournament Runner-Up
1997	9-10 Year Old	9	9	1	50.0%	"The Purple Year"
1998	11-12 Year Old	14	3	1	80.6%	Division Champion/ Tournament Champion
1999	11-12 Year Old	14	5	1	72.5%	League Champion
2000	13 Prep	9	8		52.9%	Tournament Runner-Up
2001	14-15 Year Old	18	8		69.2%	Tournament Runner-Up
2002	14-15 Year Old	19	3		86.4%	League Champion
2003	16 Prep	15	2		88.2%	League Champion/ Tournament Runner-Up
	Totals	128	44	5	73.7%	
	Percentage	72.3%	24.9%	2.8%		